NO MORE BYSTANDERS
=
NO MORE BULLIES

NO MORE BYSTANDERS

=

NO MORE BULLIES

ACTIVATING ACTION IN EDUCATIONAL PROFESSIONALS

SHONA ANDERSON

A JOINT PUBLICATION

CORWIN
A SAGE Company

ONTARIO
PRINCIPALS'
COUNCIL

For information:

Corwin
A SAGE Company
2455 Teller Road
Thousand Oaks, California 91320
(800) 233-9936
Fax: (800) 417-2466
www.corwin.com

SAGE Ltd.
1 Oliver's Yard
55 City Road
London EC1Y 1SP
United Kingdom

SAGE India Pvt. Ltd.
B 1/I 1 Mohan Cooperative
   Industrial Area
Mathura Road, New Delhi 110 044
India

SAGE Asia-Pacific Pte. Ltd.
33 Pekin Street #02-01
Far East Square
Singapore 048763

Printed in the United States of America

Library of Congress Cataloging-in-Publication Data

Anderson, Shona.
No more bystanders = No more bullies: activating action in educational professionals / Shona Anderson.
       p. cm.
"A Joint Publication With Ontario Principals' Council."
Includes bibliographical references and index.
ISBN 978-1-4129-9096-7 (pbk.)
    1. Bullying in schools—Prevention. 2. Action research in education. 3. Teachers—Training of. I. Title.

LB3013.3.A545 2011
371.5′8—dc22   2010045951

This book is printed on acid-free paper.

11   12   13   14   15   10   9   8   7   6   5   4   3   2   1

Acquisitions Editor:	Debra Stollenwerk
Associate Editor:	Desirée Bartlett
Editorial Assistant:	Kimberly Greenberg
Production Editor:	Amy Schroller
Copy Editor:	Paula L. Fleming
Typesetter:	C&M Digitals (P) Ltd.
Proofreader:	Gail Fay
Indexer:	Judy Hunt
Cover Designer:	Michael DuBowe
Permissions Editor:	Adele Hutchinson

Contents

Preface

Rationale for Writing This Book

When I first started to examine the idea of bullying in schools, I started by looking in schools. I was sitting in one of the monthly principal meetings, barely paying attention. Two of the board presenters were giving a full-day "death by PowerPoint" presentation, and all I was really thinking about was what type of muffins would be served at break. The presentation was not in itself memorable, nor was it what started me really looking at bullying. What was memorable was one of the statistics that was mentioned in passing.

The presenters talked about a study by Rona Atlas, from York University; Debra Craig, who was also working out of York University; and Wendy Pepler from Queen's University conducted in the late 1990s. Atlas, Craig, and Pepler undertook a qualitative examination of bullying in schools. They used naturalist observations to examine peer intervention in schoolyard bullying episodes. Starting with student-completed questionnaires and following up with longitudinal observations of the subjects, their observations originally focused on peer interventions and the potential role of gender differences. What they discovered through their observations with regard to educator intervention is what really caught my attention. Their observations indicated that teachers only intervened in 14 percent of classroom bullying episodes and 4 percent of playground episodes. To me this was mind-blowing.

I wasn't overly surprised by the data they collected about the playground. Bullying is very much an insidious thing that exists in hidden corners, and on most schoolyards there are many hidden corners. It was the data regarding classrooms that offended my sensibilities. My mind began to race back and go over my days in the classroom. Was it possible that I missed what was going on right in front of me? I immediately convinced myself that if they had been watching my classes, their data would have been different. I began to make up the story of how horrible and incompetent the teacher being observed must have been. That was it: they must have picked a horrible teacher to observe. I couldn't reconcile the idea that bullying would take place in my classroom with my students, the students whom I knew inside and out. While one part of my brain tried to console my conscience, the other part was asking how I could be oblivious to bullying happening right in my own classroom. The figure 14 percent seemed ludicrously impossible. It was my shock at the statistics that jarred me into really thinking about bullying and, specifically, the role that I played as a teacher.

I started off still wanting to disprove the research and questioning how it could be right. I began thinking back over all the classes that I had taught and wondering what the researchers would have found if they had been observing me. I wondered if the researchers had overreacted to incidents that were not really bullying. My questions sprang from my doubts, but as I dug into the research, I soon found that the methodology was sound. Craig, Pepler, and Atlas (2000) had a good-size sample group: 616, 762, and 535, respectively, in each of the three years of the study in two different schools with students in a variety of ages ranging from 6 to 12. They had 125 hours of playground observation and audio/visual recordings of all of the interactions. They also had a three-stage system to identify bullying acts. Their research was sound, but the teacher in me desperately wanted it to be wrong. However, the more I probed, the more I found that it wasn't.

As I Googled my way through the Internet, I quickly found that I was not the only person to look at educator or teacher intervention in bullying episodes. Study after study kept taking me back to the same place. Studies of Toronto schools found that a bullying act occurs every seven seconds but teachers were only aware of 4 percent of the incidents (Craig et al., 2000). Each time I read a statistic, I put myself in the place of the teacher being observed and really struggled with the idea that I missed things. I knew that I would never intentionally let a student in my class be bullied. I knew that my friends and colleagues would not deliberately ignore a student being mistreated. The disconnect between knowing that educators genuinely care about the students in their classes and yet are so unaware of things that are occurring in their classrooms and the school at large became the starting point for my own foray into educational research. As I examined the idea of educational professionals as bystanders in bullying episodes, I worked in conjunction with Charles Sturt University in Australia and the Bluewater District School Board in Ontario, Canada.

My research brought me to the same end point all the other researchers had arrived at. I confirmed for myself that, as educators, we are still woefully unaware of the interactions among our students (see Resource A for my 2008 article presenting this research and Resource B for the survey instrument I used). What I didn't discover was an understanding of why, a real understanding of why the data said one thing while I could not imagine a teacher ignoring a student in need or a student being mistreated. I was left with this question: How can caring adults, dedicated to children and young people, not see what is right in front of them? This book is my attempt to unravel this question.

THE CENTRAL PURPOSE OF THE BOOK

This book is designed to provide administrators with an explanation and understanding of the bystander effect through the use of narrative and research data. I have gone beyond the field of education to draw ideas from the social sciences. The narratives are either personal anecdotes or recountings of social science research or studies that illustrate the larger context of bystanderism.

The content of the book is a balance between the "broad brush" of theory with applicable hands-on activities, the latter included at the end of each chapter. The activities are designed to help administrators introduce the action items during their staff meetings or divisional meetings and include warm-up, main, exit, extension, and follow-up activities. The activities are created with the purpose of removing the attitudinal and structural barriers that cause educational professionals to be bystanders rather than interveners. They are written to reflect good pedagogical practice and incorporate a variety of teaching styles and group activities.

The warm-up section of each activity is designed to start conversations among staff members by having them either complete part of a survey or engage in a focused discussion. The main activities are generally more interactive and use different group work techniques. The exit activities are reflective and allow individuals to think deeply about what they have learned and how they will change their practice. The follow-up activities are designed to be used by a small group of educational professionals who would be responsible for reviewing the exit activity information. Ideally, each school would create a "safe schools team" with representatives from all stakeholders in the school to use the follow-up activities effectively. A Safe Schools Team, along the lines of those used in Ontario, is the ideal, as it helps to diffuse responsibility for bullying prevention from being exclusively that of the school administrators to a shared responsibility of all staff members.

THE APPROACH OF THE BOOK

The book is designed to be used in one of two ways, depending on the needs of the reader.

1. It can be read sequentially in the traditional cover-to-cover manner.

2. Since no two schools or readers are at the same point, readers can also use the "pulse check" at the end of the introduction to allow them to differentiate their reading based on their own needs. The questions in the pulse check will allow the reader to jump to the section that targets the weaknesses on which they want to focus.

While the book is a cohesive unit and each idea and activity links to the whole in a sequential manner, it is also written in a way to allow each chapter to stand alone or to be used in a nonsequential manner if doing so better suits the needs of the reader.

As you read this book, you will be guided by a Continuum to Action. This Continuum to Action will guide your learning through three phases:

1. Pre-bystanderism

2. Decision making

3. Post-bystanderism

The three phases of the Continuum to Action, which are subdivided into seven key elements, provide the framework for this book.

SPECIAL FEATURES

This book contains many different special features, which are woven into each chapter. The special features are designed to be catalysts for thinking, discussion, and—most importantly—action.

Pulse Check in the Introduction

The purpose of the "pulse check" is to allow readers to differentiate the text to meet their particular needs. The book is designed to follow the continuum sequentially; however, each section can be used in a stand-alone manner to target the immediate learning need of the reader.

Action Items

The purpose of the action items is to allow readers to engage their learning in action through a preplanned and scripted activity. The action items are designed to model good teaching pedagogy to allow school administrators to use them, as is, during a staff meeting as a learning activity for the entire staff. Each action section includes a warm-up activity, the main activity with extensions and variations, an exit activity, and follow-up actions. They incorporate good teaching strategies with different elements of group work to help facilitate peer-to-peer learning and ownership of the understandings. While the activities need to be coordinated, presumably by the school administrator, they are not "lessons" to be delivered. Rather, they are opportunities to facilitate discussions to improve the understanding of everyone. Again each part of the action item can stand alone to accommodate the time constraints of busy school life. Following are the action items:

- Fact or Myth?
- Identify Hot Spots
- Dotmocracy
- Math, Math, and Even More Math
- Super Supervision
- A Common Language
- Character Counts
- Communication 101

Reflection Points and Guiding Questions in Each Chapter

The reflection points and guiding questions throughout the chapters are designed to provoke the readers' thinking and personal reflections as to their own roles in the bystander cycle. These points can also be used as guiding questions and discussion points for small groups or a book study group.

Case Studies

Case studies at the end of every chapter are designed to provoke self-reflection and discussion. They vary in length and depth of detail and at times purposely use stereotypical description of people or scenarios. The students/adults/situations in the case studies are composites of several different students/adults/situations, and all of the names have been changed. The purpose of the case studies is to help educational professionals think through scenarios so that when they encounter them in reality, they have prethought their actions.

This book is unlike the myriad of other books on bullying because it focuses on an important paradigm shift. Through reading the theories and research, the case studies and narratives, you will begin to shift your thinking about how to address bullying from focusing exclusively on the students in your school to include an intentional, purposeful, and transparent focus on educational professionals. This book will help you

- develop a deeper understanding of the elements of bystanderism in educational professionals through framing the ideas in the larger realm of social sciences.
- provide you with tangible actions that are designed to address the seven stages of the bystander decision-making cycle for schools. Each chapter focuses on different aspects of bystanderism and ends with an action activity.
- broaden your thinking through case studies and self-reflection prompts included in every chapter.

It is important to note that this book is not a panacea and that there is no "one size fits all" answer when it comes to bullying and bystanderism. The self-reflections, the case studies, and the activities do not come with an answer key because there is no "correct" answer. More important than the answer is the thinking. The self-reflections are designed to provoke some self-analysis and conversations among the educational professionals in each school.

Acknowledgments

This book came about as a result of a combination of timing, luck, and sleep deprivation. The arrival of my twins changed my world in so many ways I can't even remember life before January 18, 2008. One of the biggest changes, along with the fact that I can now do most things in life while holding two kids, was the lack of sleep that comes with twins. For months I don't remember sleeping. I must have slept, but I don't remember it. I do remember 18 bottles and 18 diaper changes every day for what seemed like forever. I also remember my mom being there and finally understanding her in a way that I never had before. It was somewhere into the second or third month of feedings and changes every two to three hours that I was sitting in my sunroom, barely conscious, with a baby in both arms, watching television and hoping that one or both of them would fall asleep again, that luck and timing happened.

By sheer luck I had turned the television onto CBC, and *The Hour* with George Stroumboulopoulos was just coming on. At the time it was not a show that I ever watched, although now I try to catch it whenever I can. One of his guests that day was Malcolm Gladwell; I had never heard of him, but now I am obsessed with his writing. The luck of being awake at 4:00 A.M. and watching a show that I never watched to hear an author whom I had never heard of speak about his new book was a great twist of fate.

I was too tired to really understand the depth of Gladwell, and I'm not certain even when I'm well rested and fully awake that my mind can keep up with him, but I tucked away his name and the title *Outliers*. Months later the twins began sleeping a bit better, and I began to manage thoughts that went beyond sheer survival. I listened to *Outliers*, followed by *The Tipping Point* and *Blink*. I was blown away by each book, and for the first time I really began to think outside the narrow confines of education.

As a result the acknowledgment for the inspiration for this book goes to four people, two of whom I know and two of whom I've never met. Zoe and Ewan were the catalyst, George Stroumboulopoulos was the link, and Malcolm Gladwell was the intellectual trigger.

In addition, some very important people supported me in making my ideas reality. First and foremost, my parents have been constant, positive guiding influences in my life. I never really understood the depth of their commitment until I had the privilege of watching them with their grand-children. Grandma Bel and Papa are full-time, hands-on grandparents, and it is through their support that I am able to balance the demands of working full-time and being a parent. My in-laws are also phenomenally loving grandparents who take amazing care of my twins. My husband, despite being a workaholic himself, finds time to listen to my rants, gives our twins baths, and puts up with my awful taste in television shows. My friends have also been a constant support system and inspiration. They keep me grounded and encourage me to reach for the stars at the same time.

In my professional life I have been lucky enough to work with some ter-rific educators who have mentored my growth both as a professional and as a person. The Bluewater District School Board has provided me with many learning opportunities. The Ontario Principals' Council, specifically Joanne Robinson, has also supported my work over the past four years.

Many of the fabulous things in my life also could not have happened without the work of some incredible doctors. My diagnosis with lupus and rheumatoid arthritis more than ten years ago was life changing. Since then Dr. Denberg, Dr. Pillersdorf, and Dr. Wasserman of McMaster Hospital in Hamilton, Ontario, have been instrumental in me living a nor-mal life. McMaster's high-risk obstetrics clinic also monitored my preg-nancy and ensured that both my twins arrived healthy and happy.

The writing of this book has been a fascinating experience beyond anything I imagined it would be. I have developed as a writer and been pushed to think at a level that I did not realize that I could. My editor, Deb Stollenwerk, has been an incredibly positive guide throughout the entire process. Her feedback and thoughts have been invaluable.

Publisher's Acknowledgments

Corwin gratefully acknowledges the comments and editorial insight from the following individuals:

Melanie Mares, Academic Coach
Lowndes Middle School
Valdosta, GA

Chris Sarellas, Principal
Vaughan Secondary School
Thornhill, Ontario, Canada

Janice Nicholls, Principal
Spruce Ridge Community School
Bluewater District School Board
Durham, Ontario

Kim E. Vogel, Principal
Parkdale Elementary School
Parkdale, OR

About the Author

 **Shona Anderson** has been an educator since 1996. She started her teaching career with the Upper Grand District School Board as a core French teacher. She began taking Additional Qualifications courses and holds a double specialization in the teaching of French as a Second Language and Computers in the Classroom. Her work as both an English teacher and a French teacher led her to administration in 2003 for the Bluewater District School Board. Working in schools as both an administrator and a teacher has been a rewarding experience, allowing Shona to learn from children and adults alike. Shona is also a part-time faculty member of the University of Western Ontario.

Shona holds a BA in English from the University of Guelph and a Post Graduate Certificate in Education in secondary education from the University of Strathclyde in Glasgow, Scotland. Shona also completed her Master of Education through Charles Sturt University in Australia with a focus on educational research in the area of bullying. Her research was supported by the Ontario Principals' Council (OPC), and she has both written for its publication, called the *Register*, and presented at the annual Odyssey conference. Shona has also published an action manual for administrators called *Creating a Culture of Action* for OPC.

Outside of school Shona is a very busy mother of two-year-old twins, Zoe and Ewan. Shona is a self-professed reality television junkie.

Please visit www.shonaanderson.com for more information regarding the author, as well as additional resources and case studies.

To Zoe and Ewan

I'll love you forever. I'll like you for always.
As long as I'm living my babies you'll be.

—Robert Munsch, 1995

Mom

Introduction

Bullying and Bystanderism

IF WE DO WHAT WE'VE ALWAYS DONE, WE'LL GET WHAT WE'VE ALWAYS GOTTEN

Bullying has been an acknowledged problem in schools for decades, and for just as long educators have been trying to find solutions. Schools have spent a great deal of time and money on various antibullying programs and, more recently, character education in an attempt to stop bullying behavior. Despite our best efforts, however, bullying continues to be a global dilemma. The statistics are consistent and tell the same story in country after country, school after school. Bullying exists and is a daily occurrence for many of our students.

- Research conducted in Canada, Europe, and the United States has shown that roughly 10 to 15 percent of students aged 11 to 15 admitted being involved in weekly physical bullying (Craig & Harel, 2004; Duncan, 1999; Sourander, Helstela, Helenius, & Piha, 2000).
- Bullying is a common problem worldwide affecting one in five school-aged children. The proportion of school-aged children who report being bullied is consistent across countries: Australia (17%), England (19%), Japan (15%), Norway (14%), Spain (17%), and United States (16%; Weir, 2001).
- A survey was administered to 4,763 Canadian children in Grades 1 to 8, and 6 percent admitted bullying others, 15 percent reported being victimized, and 2 percent reported being both bullies and victims (Pepler & Craig, 1997).
- Every month, 13 percent of Canadian students report being victims of electronic bullying or of electronically bullying others (Canadian Public Health Association, 2004).

- One in ten teenagers is a victim of cyber bullying in the United Kingdom (MSN, 2006).
- Thirty-nine percent of middle schoolers and 36 percent of high schoolers say they don't feel safe at schools (Josephson Institute, 2001).

Despite all of the programs and lessons, the problem has not disappeared. In fact, bullying has evolved in ways that were not even imagined 40 years ago when Dan Olweus, a Norwegian researcher who is commonly known as the grandfather of the antibullying initiative, started his investigations. Bullying is evolving with a Darwinistic perseverance to thrive. The classic schoolyard bully who takes your lunch money is now almost a welcome and easily dealt with problem. The new breeds of bully that have evolved are nearly invisible, as the anonymity of computers allows cyber bullying to be imperceptible.

When we talk about bullying in schools, it is very comfortable to discuss the actions of the students. As educators, we use the terms *bully* and *victim* with a fair degree of ease. For the past 30 years, the word *bullying* has been part of the common vernacular of teaching. Dan Olweus developed the first formal definition of *bullying* in the 1970s. His extensive work over the past four decades has allowed his definition to evolve to characterize bullying as intentional, repeated, hurtful acts, words, or other behavior, such as name-calling, threatening, and/or shunning, committed by one or more children against another child (Olweus, 2001).

Students often self-identify as both the bullied and the bully (Nansel et al., 2004) making intervention difficult from a third party perspective. In 1978 Olweus began to define bullying and described three types of bully: the aggressive bully, the passive bully, and the bully-victim. Stephenson and Smith (1989) also identified three types of bullies: physical, verbal, and emotional. The concept of bullying has evolved to now include nine subcategories of bullying: physical, verbal, social or relational, reactive-victim, cyber or electronic, gender-based, racial or ethnocultural, sexual, and religious, as well as multiple types of victims generally categorized as passive and aggressive (see Resource C for definitions). In all cases, the actions of the bully are purposeful and intended to hurt or upset the victim.

While all forms of bullying have the same end goal, they are very different in their approaches and therefore in their observability. A hit, trip, or punch is easy to see, while the subtleties of social bullying, such as a raised eyebrow or a quiet whisper, are relatively inconspicuous. Verbal and social bullying are the most difficult to stop, as they are the most challenging for educational professionals to observe (Macklem, 2003). They can occur in as little as seven seconds, and social bullies are experts in timing and nuance (Craig & Pepler, 2003). The subtleties of the differences between teasing and taunting allow bullies to disguise the maliciousness of their actions to any third-party observers.

Craig and Pepler (2003) highlighted the differences between teasing and taunting. Teasing is determined to be a normal part of friendships and friendship groups, while taunting is not acceptable and is a form of bullying. Teasing is fun and innocent in nature; all the people involved are laughing. Taunting, on the other hand, is one-sided and does not make the relationship better. Unfortunately, to an outsider the differences can often be difficult to detect. What an observer sees, how the victim feels, and what the bully intends may be very different. Coloroso (2003) clarified the difference between the two. While the differences are subtle, they are essential for the bystander to understand, as bullies will often say they are just teasing when in truth their intent is cruel.

Olweus began examining bullying as a didactic interaction between the bully and the victim. Traditionally, discussions around bullying focus on a dichotomous relationship between the perpetrator and the victim. This view ignores the role of the bystander, who is present in 85 percent of bullying incidents (Craig & Pepler, 1997). Craig and Pepler found that having other children watching factored strongly in whether the bullying incident occurred, and once it did occur, these peers affected the final outcome. Indeed, as O'Connell, Pepler, and Craig (1999) concurred, peers are documented as being present in as many as 85 percent of bullying episodes. In fact, O'Connell et al. determined that in 81 percent of bullying episodes, peers actually reinforced the negative behaviors, only intervening in 13 percent of the episodes. Moreover, when the bystander did intervene, it was often in a socially inappropriate manner, such as by pushing or shoving the people involved rather than using words or getting help from a teacher nearby. The "group context is especially relevant" (Salmivalli, 2001, p. 400) to problem solving and deterring bullying. The acknowledgment of a third-party role has changed the way that researchers and educational professionals view bullying episodes.

Not until the late 1990s did the dyad become a triad with the introduction of the bystander. Olweus (1993) found that peers are invariably involved in bullying. Peers can act as henchmen for the bully, peers can be neutral, peers can be disengaged onlookers, or peers can be seen as actively helping or defending the victim (Olweus). To blur further the tridactic relationships of bullying, the roles are at times interchangeable. For example, the student who is typically the bully can be either the bullied or the bystander, and vice versa. While at times the roles are interchangeable, researchers have attempted to clarify each role. The role of the bullied, traditionally known as the victim, has been defined by many researchers.

However, Coloroso (2003) put forward the more recent and complete definition. The *bullied* is the person who repeatedly receives the attention of the bully in the form of negative behavior. The targeted behaviors of the bully cause fear, distress, or harm to the bullied.

The most recently explored aspect of bullying, and the focus of this book, is that of the bystander. The definition is evolving, although the role has been acknowledged since the late 1990s. Olweus (1993) defined the *bystander* as an individual who is present but does not take part in the situation or event. As educators, we use these terms in reference to students with relative ease. The child-centric perspective has been the prevalent one when thinking about the bully, the bullied, and the bystander. Our comfort level changes when we begin to think of ourselves in these terms.

THE CONTINUUM TO ACTION

The Continuum to Action organizes our knowledge regarding the power of bystander intervention and our knowledge regarding the educational professional and bystanderism. Studies by Craig and Pepler (1997) demonstrated that bullying episodes occur every 7 minutes on the playground and every 25 minutes in the classrooms. These researchers also found that bullying episodes stop in less than ten seconds 57 percent of the time when someone intervenes on behalf of the victim. In 2000 Craig, Pepler, and Atlas found that educational professionals only intervene in 4 percent of bullying episodes.

Bystanders, according to Coloroso (2003), are people who stand idly by when bullying occurs or sometimes ignore bullying and as a result are not innocent in the bullying cycle. Typically, a bystander is thought to be a peer. The work of Craig et al. (2000) framed educators as bystanders in the same terms as Coloroso (2003) defined student bystanders, as they were observed to be idle in over 80 percent of bullying episodes. Educational professionals are therefore defined as bystanders when they are idle in the bullying cycle.

Bystander Cycle

The *bystander cycle*, based in traditional bystander research by Huston, Ruggiero, Conner, and Geis (1981), determined that being idle can occur at five points in the intervention process.

1. Noticing that something unusual is going on

2. Deciding that something is indeed out of the ordinary

3. Determining the extent to which one is responsible for helping

4. Determining whether one has the skills to help

5. Deciding whether or not to help the person in need

Extending the Bystander Cycle Within the Continuum to Action

This book will frame the traditional five stages of bystander intervention within the Continuum to Action. The Continuum to Action extends the traditional five stages into a trisected seven-stage continuum. The pre-bystandersim stage supports the movement of the educational professional to action through the creation of a vehicle for understanding bystanderism and one's own behaviors. The proactive, decision-making section of the spectrum is designed to motivate intentional actions. Finally, the post-bystanderism stage extends the incident and interactions into a clearly communicated learning experience, which creates a new common understanding.

Pre-Bystanderism

The pre-bystanderism stage of the Continuum to Action occurs before the educational professional enters the decision-making stage, because it is through the self-reflection that occurs here that he or she will be able to notice that something unusual is going on. In the pre-bystanderism part of the continuum, the educational professional examines his or her own beliefs and adjusts the paradigms of perception.

Decision Making

Decision making is the part of the Continuum to Action that occurs in the moment. It is comprised of a series of four small decisions. Educational professionals very quickly need to decide that something is out of the ordinary, determine their level of responsibility, and decide if they have the skills to help before making the final decision of whether or not to help.

Post-Bystanderism

The post-bystanderism end of the spectrum allows the educational professional to extend the action of intervening into a "teachable moment" through clearly communicating with the people involved, including the other students present and the parent community. Closing the communication gap is a very powerful tool for transforming a negative incident into a learning moment.

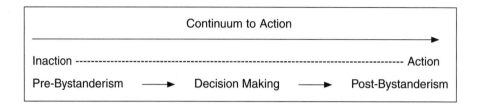

- Pre-bystanderism—To be able to notice that something unusual is going on
  1. Understand personal primed perceptions.
  2. Remove altruistic blind spots.

- Decision making—The rapid decisions that need to occur in the moment
  3. Decide that something is indeed out of the ordinary.
  4. Determine the extent to which one is responsible for helping.
  5. Determine whether one has the skills to help.
  6. Decide whether or not to help the person in need.

- Post-bystanderism—Essential step for schools that follows helping the person in need
  7. Close the communication gap.

THE ELEPHANT IN THE ROOM

While the definition of the *bystander* is inclusive of everyone, it was the work of Craig and Pepler (2003) that suggested that educational professionals be framed clearly with this label. The labeling of educators as bystanders is a huge elephant that no one wants to acknowledge because it does not match with our beliefs about teachers. It is incredibly uncomfortable to think that the adults to whom we trust our children on a daily basis are standing by and doing nothing while bullying occurs. The teacher in me has great difficulty thinking these thoughts, let alone putting them down in writing. It needs to be acknowledged at this point that I do not believe that the majority of teachers are purposefully bystanders. My research clearly found that it is lack of knowledge, not lack of good intentions, that creates bystanderism in educators. My data, which the chapters of this book will examine more in depth, showed that the most prevalent reason for not intervening is not lack of caring but lack of awareness. Of respondents, 80 percent indicated that this is the number one reason that they do not intervene in bullying episodes. I truly believe in the good of teachers and that they are doing the best they can to manage in increasingly complex and demanding settings. That said, I also embrace the idea expressed by Maya Angelou: "You did then what you knew how to do; and when you knew better, you did better." By acknowledging the elephant and examining it closely, we can know better and ultimately do better.

Thin Slicing the Bystander Cycle

The art of "thin slicing" is the ability to examine something, an incident or an action, in slivers. Malcolm Gladwell argued in *Blink* (2005) that our intuitive knowledge can be developed through experience, training, and knowledge. Through thin slicing bystanderism, we can determine what to target for educators to improve their natural instincts and reactions. Thin slicing something as complex as bystanderism allows us to develop a better understanding of all the layers and ideas contained within. Thin slicing also allows for the ability to analyze a concept with greater depth and to target actions and solutions with more precision. It lets us scrutinize the many subdecisions that occur in what on the surface appears to be one simple act.

Bystanderism on the surface appears to be one simple decision. Through thin slicing bystanderism, however, one realizes that it is a collection of a series of five small decisions that occur in rapid succession to create either action or inaction. Huston et al. (1981) parsed bystanderism by considering five slices:

Slice 1: Notice that something unusual is going on.

Slice 2: Decide that something is indeed out of the ordinary.

Slice 3: Determine the extent to which one has the responsibility to help.

Slice 4: Determine whether one has the skill to help.

Slice 5: Decide whether or not to aid the person in need.

Slice 1

Slice 1 is to notice that something unusual is going on. Epp and Epp (2000) found that this is often difficult for educational professionals as a result of a strong code of silence among students related to bullying. In 2000, Pepler and Craig's research supported the conclusions of Epp and Epp when they found that 53 percent of students did not tell a teacher about being bullied, 37 percent did not tell their parents about it, and 28 percent told no one at all. Reasons most often given for not reporting were that the victim did not want to make things worse, the victim felt the problem was not serious enough, or the victim did not want the hassle (Joong & Ridler, 2005). The code of silence has the ability to stop the cycle of intervention at the first slice, as often the subtlety of social bullying makes it very difficult to observe and the bystander may not notice that something unusual, bullying, is occurring.

Slice 2

Slice 2 occurs when a bystander decides that something is indeed out of the ordinary. He or she must then decide whether something is wrong and if help is needed. Sorting out which behaviors constitute bullying is a difficult process and can contribute to a lack of intervention in bullying situations (Hazler, 1998; Hazler, Miller, Carney, & Green, 2001). It would appear that indirect bullying is particularly challenging for teachers to recognize and that they have difficulty knowing whether and how to intervene in this type of bullying. It seems that the element of subjectivity, or how educational professionals have been primed, affects their ability to "see" bullying. As Craig et al. (2000) found, teachers characterize incidents differently depending on their own definition of bullying. Several studies demonstrate that many teachers referred to subjectivity, particularly with regard to indirect bullying (Ireland & Ireland, 2000; Siann, Callaghan, Lockhart, & Rawson, 1993). Underestimating the harm caused by forms of bullying such as nonviolent victimization may lead to an inappropriate response, which can amount to further victimization (Astor, 1995).

Slice 3

Once the situation is defined by the bystander, slice 3 is the mini decision to determine the extent to which one has the responsibility to help. In one study, Boulton (1997) elicited teachers' attitudes toward bullying and their beliefs about their ability to deal with bullying. Boulton found that most of the teachers considered physical assaults and threats bullying, but a significant proportion did not view behaviors such as exclusion or name-calling as bullying. Townsend-Wiggins (2001) came to a similar conclusion when she established that teachers' understanding of bullying, particularly relational bullying, was limited. Nicolaides, Toda, and Smith (2002) conducted a study on teacher candidates' knowledge and attitudes regarding bullying, their views on the significance of bullying, and their confidence in dealing with bullying. The respondents depicted bullies as having low self-esteem and lacking social skills, which contradicts emerging evidence that some bullies actually "may be quite socially skilled, adept manipulators of the social environment who can get rewards from bullying more vulnerable peers" (Nicolaides et al., p. 115). A growing body of literature indicates that educational professionals are not comfortable with or capable of intervening consistently and effectively (Bolton, 1997; Craig & Pepler, 2003; Dawkins & Hill, 1995; Mishna, 2004; Rigby & Bagshaw, 2003). Teachers' understanding may well determine whether they see an incident as bullying and whether they intervene appropriately (Boulton). Some educational professionals make assumptions about characteristics that victims will display with regard to their appearance or social abilities, and these assumptions seem to prevent them from recognizing victimized children who do not match them (Rigby & Bagshaw).

Intertwined with subjectivity is empathy, which emerged as a theme that appeared to influence how teachers responded to the children who were identified as bullied (Rigby & Bagshaw, 2003). Other research has similarly found an association between teachers' empathy for the bullied child and their responses (Craig et al., 2000; Kallestad & Olweus, 2003). For example, teachers who experienced a similar event in their own lives were more likely to respond and intervene on behalf of the bullied. However, teachers who did not have a positive perception of the bullied student were more likely to remain unresponsive to the situation (Twemlow, Fonagy, & Sacco, 2004).

It would appear from the current literature that a large amount of bullying behavior occurs in the classroom or other school settings where adults are present to observe and intervene (Swearer, Song, Cary, Eagle, & Mickelson, 2001). Teachers tend to underestimate bullying and do little to discourage it (Olweus, 1993), and a lack of consistent discipline for bullying reinforces the belief that such aggressive acts will achieve a desired goal without negative consequences (Howard, Horne, & Joliff, 2002). Teachers said they almost always intervened 71 percent of the time, while students said that intervention occurred only 25 percent of the time (Pepler & Craig, 2000). Studies also indicate that teachers intervene in 14 percent of classroom episodes and in only 4 percent of school ground episodes (Pepler & Craig). The work of Epp and Epp (1998) supported the findings of Pepler and Craig; their research determined that students reported that teachers should be more aware of and responsive to bullying itself or complaints of bullying. Through their interviews with students, Pepler and Craig determined that 42 percent of bullies and 46 percent of victims report that they have talked to teachers about problems related to bullying. Of the victims who did report the incident, most felt that nothing was done and were dissatisfied with how the episode was handled (Joong & Ridler, 2005). Developing an awareness of the complexity of this phenomenon may lead teachers to become "more vigilant and responsive to bullying problems which, in turn, may give children more confidence to seek teachers' assistance when bullying occurs" (Atlas & Pepler, 1998, p. 94).

Slice 4

When the bystander assumes responsibility for helping the victim and moves into slice 4 of the decision, the bystander must decide whether he or she possesses the appropriate form of help to render. Educational professionals have various levels of training with regard to bullying. In fact, most of their training comes from reading the teachers' guides that accompany whatever program they are using to teach their students. They are somewhat trained on how to teach students about their roles but have very limited training directly related to their own roles and actions. Educational professionals need training that is specifically targeted to help them overcome the dilemma of not wanting to make things worse. In the moment, when they observe a bullying situation, they need to decide whether or not they have the skills to make a difference. Telling a student to stop is a very limited way to make an intervention, yet it is the only way most educators are aware of. The appropriate forms of help one can give are multifaceted. Therefore, slice 4 poses a very difficult mini question for most educators to answer with confidence.

Slice 5

Finally in slice 5, after the bystander has progressed rapidly through the four previous sections of this decision, he or she must decide whether or not to aid the person in need (Huston et al., 1981). Most antibullying education programs have focused on how to empower student bystanders, and while this is an important aspect of antibullying education, that alone will not change the cycle (Atlas & Pepler, 1998).

It is important for educational professionals to recognize that how they understand and respond to bullying can have an effect on their students. According to the Northwest Regional Educational Laboratory "teachers need to understand that their response to bullying makes a difference" (2001, p. 10). Doubting a child's view may contribute to his or her lack of disclosure to teachers or any other educational professional (Dawkins & Hill, 1995; Mishna, 2004). Those involved in bullying (bullies, the bullied, and bystanders) are likely to have more negative opinions of a teacher's capacity to resolve conflicts (Rigby & Bagshaw, 2003). Despite the importance of intervention, Mishna, Scarcello, Pepler, and Wiener (2005) determined that teachers often remain in the early stages of the decision to intervene when they are unaware that a child feels bullied; they therefore do not consider the situation serious and do not respond appropriately.

One of the tools that teachers have been given to support them in bullying situations comes in the form of antibullying programs. These programs have taken on many forms and labels since they were introduced in the early 1970s. According to Mishna et al. (2005) many teachers surveyed felt that they were not capable of delivering all the curricular requirements and addressing bullying concerns on a daily basis. The addition of another element to an already full day has left teachers feeling pressure and stress regarding student behavior (Hazler, 1998). Furthermore, it has been difficult to choose which programs teachers should spend their time and energy implementing, as identifying which programs have actually resulted in a decrease in school violence has proven difficult (Schultz & Da Costa, 2005). Rigby (1998) found that regardless of what program is used, when all members of the school community are supportive, the success rate can be as high as 60 to 70 percent. Unfortunately, educational professionals struggle to know what their role is and how to support students due to the lack of alignment between existing school policies and guidelines, inconsistent systemic support, and distinguishing between "normal" and bullying behaviors (Mishna et al., 2005).

Two More Slices in the Continuum to Action

The five slices just detailed are the five mini decisions that need to be made to create action in the world outside of education, but they are only part of the process needed to create action within the world of schools. The Continuum to Action incorporates the five slices but it expands beyond the cycle in both directions. The Continuum to Action includes two pre-bystanderism slices necessary to allow education professionals to begin to understand their role within the bullying tridactic relationship. The post-bystanderism slice is also important within the school setting, as it addresses the need for communication that exists both within schools themselves and with their extended communities.

Within the pre-bystanderism section of the Continuum to Action, educational professionals need to be reflective practitioners to begin to understand their own biases and perceptions regarding bullying. The first stage of the continuum addresses how personal histories and experiences prime our perceptions, making it challenging to see situations as they are. The second stage in the pre-bystanderism section focuses on helping educational professionals remove their own barriers to action by creating an understanding of their own altruistic blind spots. This self-reflective phase leads into the decision-making section of the continuum, which occurs in the moment. This is comprised of the original components of the bystander intervention cycle created by Huston et al. (1981). Finally, the post-bystanderism phase addresses the communication of actions at the end of the bullying episode. It acknowledges that in schools, bullying does not end when the incident ends but when, through good communication, learning occurs and a common understanding is reached.

TURNING ON THE LIGHTS

The Continuum to Action is like turning a light switch. Once you begin to be a truly reflective practitioner regarding your own beliefs and actions, you will be able to see your path to action lit clearly before you.

We have all experienced the shock to our systems when, first thing in the morning after a peaceful night's sleep, the lights are suddenly turned on. The next time it happens, try to be conscious of your own reaction. There is an immediate instinct to close your eyes and turn away quickly. Your body reacts as if it is in pain. Your face visibly squints and flinches. Once you get through the initial discomfort and your eyes adjust, you realize that you can see and function so much more effectively with the lights on than you could stumbling around in the dark.

Turning on the lights and examining bullying through the lens of radical transparency and honesty invokes the same instinct to close your eyes and turn away quickly. The initial discomfort of acknowledging that what we have been doing hasn't been working and the pain of self-reflection is only temporary, however. Once our eyes adjust to the truth of the current situation, we can see and function much more effectively for the benefit of our students. As U.S. Supreme Court Justice Louis Brandeis famously put it, "Sunlight is the best disinfectant." The blinding brightness of sunlight allows us to see the real truths about our own roles in bullying and thereby begin the process to remove the shadows in which bullying thrives.

ACTION: PULSE CHECK

How is the heartbeat of your school? Consider the following questions with regard to yourself, your school, and the school's individual needs. You may wish to consider them by yourself, in conjunction with your Safe Schools Team, or with your entire staff. If you feel that you or your staff are already knowledgeable in a particular area, you may choose to skip the suggested chapter(s) and related activities. However, if you answer no to any of the questions, you can read the suggested chapter and complete the suggested activities to target specific weaknesses.

1. Do you have a Safe Schools Team at your school?

   Yes   No—Go to Chapter 1 on page 15.

2. Have you and your entire staff (teachers, educational assistants, office professionals, and custodians) received antibullying and character education training?

   Yes   No—Go to the Decision Making section on pages 55–86.

3. Do you and your entire staff have a common language to use when discussing bullying?

   Yes   No—Go to Chapter 7 on page 89.

4. Do you and your entire staff have a good understanding of where and when bullying occurs in your school?

   Yes   No—Go to Chapter 3 on page 39.

5. Do you and your entire staff have a solid understanding of your expectations with regard to active student supervision?

   Yes   No—Go to Chapter 6 on page 77.

6. Do you and your entire staff know your procedures for reporting incidents to the office?

   Yes   No—Go to Chapter 7 on page 89.

7. Do you and your entire staff know what behaviors are unacceptable and which ones are desirable?

   Yes   No—Go to Chapter 4 on page 55.

8. Do you have new staff members who are not familiar with your school's expectations?

   Yes   No—Go to the Decision Making section on page 55.

9. Has your Safe Schools Team been effective since its formation?

   Yes   No—Go to Chapter 8 on page 97.

(Continued)

(Continued)

   10. Do you and your staff have a common understanding of how to communicate effectively with your parent community?

       Yes   No—Go to Chapter 9 on page 109.

   11. Do you and your staff have a common belief system with regard to bullying?

       Yes   No—Go to Chapter 8 on page 23.

The Team Approach
to Safe Schools

Throughout this book I refer to a school-based Safe Schools Team. This committee, legally required in Ontario, goes beyond the traditional anti-bullying committees that exist in some form or another in many schools. A Safe Schools Team is not required in order to implement any or all of the ideas in this book, but this evolved team format does have advantages.

You will also notice that in each chapter I refer to the Safe Schools Team as coordinating "action" activities, including being responsible for follow-up to the activities. This serves two purposes: (1) having someone or some group responsible for follow-up ensures that some follow-through occurs, and (2) having the team oversee follow-up ensures that the responsibility for keeping the school safe is diffused and does not rest solely on the principal's shoulders.

In this chapter I outline a very brief history of the evolution of the Safe Schools legislation in Ontario and discuss how to create a Safe Schools Team.

WHAT IS A SAFE SCHOOLS TEAM?

In November 2005 the Ontario government, after extensive consultation, put forward a comprehensive list of recommendations, one of which was to establish a Safe Schools Team. It was suggested that the team meet at least three times per year and that the team include teachers, staff members, parents, administrators, community members, and students. This was the first time such a team would include parents, community members, and students, and this inclusion of so many different shareholders was the first step in the evolution of the antibullying committees present in most schools today. It was also the first time that a committee would exist for the purpose of monitoring effectiveness rather than to organize special events. New laws and amendments, which were more detailed and explicit, were enacted in 2009 when the Education Act was amended to be Education Amendment Act (Keeping Our Kids Safe at School). The Safe Schools Team under the Ontario Ministry of Education's Policy/Program Memorandum No. 144 (PPM 144) was then reviewed, and small wording changes specified the inclusion of one nonteaching staff member and "at least" one student (where appropriate).

CREATING A SAFE SCHOOLS TEAM IN YOUR SCHOOL

Creating an effective and active Safe Schools Team is challenging and requires planning. One of the most important aspects of forming such a group of is the development of a "team" concept. The team is not simply a committee chaired by the principal; rather it is a diverse team of shareholders, all of whom need to have a voice in the process. This team is heterogeneous by definition, as the members have been included because of their diverse backgrounds and perspectives. This type of team has the potential for great synergism as it develops ideas and actions, but it also has the potential for conflict and unbalance. It is important as the principal that you establish clear norms for the group and that you have a clear understanding of the life cycle of teams first established by Tuckman (1965), which includes forming, storming, norming, and performing. While the principal has an essential and guiding role in the formation and monitoring of this group, it is preferable for another staff member to act as the chair, thus sharing the responsibility.

The thinking behind whom should be included as a member of the Safe Schools Team is a multistep process.

• **Step 1.** Examine a process for determining readiness for being a team member. It is essential that the team members are open to addressing all types of bullying and discrimination, including areas such as age, race, sexual orientation, gender, faith, disability, ethnicity, and socioeconomic status. Depending on people's experiences and perceptions, they may be at varying levels of readiness to address issues fairly. It is important that no members are volunteering to be part of this team because of personal agendas involving their child or targeting another child. You may wish to survey potential team members to determine their readiness and ensure that everyone is dedicated to building a safe, equitable, and inclusive learning environment.

• **Step 2.** Consider using some external training, either through your school board or with an external facilitator, to help with the team building and goal setting. Having external support helps place all the team members on an equal level rather than maintaining the hierarchy of principal, teaching staff, nonteaching staff, community member, and student, which can be counterproductive to the team's functioning. This external facilitator may be needed for only one or two meetings to help establish the team, or the facilitator may assist at various points throughout the life of the team.

• **Step 3.** Examine the logistics of the team and what types of infrastructure supports are required. This step is essential to ensure that the team is active and not simply a committee on paper only. In this step a plan of when, where, and for how long you will meet must be clearly delineated. Such a plan creates a committed schedule for the meetings and allows team members to prioritize them.

• **Step 4.** Establish shared and diffused responsibility. This team represents the larger school community; therefore, each team member needs a forum or format in which to consult with and inform those whom they represent. Open and consistent two-way communication between the team members and their constituents will increase the effectiveness of the team and thereby decrease bullying and other negative behaviors.

• **Step 5.** Begin with learning, not action. The team needs to begin with learning as much as it can about bullying in general but also about the climate of its own school. Just as with good teaching, diagnostic assessments are important. New legislation in Ontario requires that a climate survey take place every two years. This diagnostic assessment of staff, students, and parents is needed to ensure that the team is addressing site-specific needs and focusing its actions in a targeted manner to improve the school climate.

The five steps of thinking that need to occur before the first meeting are crucial to start off the Safe Schools Team in the right direction. The principal or school leadership team needs to give deep consideration to choosing the right staff members, both teaching and nonteaching, and the right community members and students. Once the best people are chosen to be part of the team, infrastructure is needed to optimize their effectiveness, and different team members will need different levels of support to work within the established structures. For example, student representatives, depending on their age, may need substantial guidance to be successful team members.

CASE STUDY: WHO'S ON YOUR TEAM?

Read the brief biographies of the potential team members below and try to determine whom you would want on your Safe Schools Team. Remember, you need a teaching and a nonteaching staff member, as well as a community representative and a student representative.

You are the principal of a junior kindergarten (JK) to Grade 8 dual-track (French immersion and English) school with a student population of approximately 450 students. You began in January by tracking the incidents that come to the office, and it is now March. You have had over 120 incidents for which you could have considered suspension, but you have issued suspensions in only 10 percent of the cases. Of those 12 suspensions, 10 were for one day, 1 was for three days, and 1 is currently in an expulsion process. You know that bullying is a problem in your school, and you are selecting members for your Safe School Team.

Case Study Team Table

Name	Role	Experience	Other
Mr. Blue	Teacher	35 years—Grade 2	2 grown children—divorced 3 times—Caucasian
Mr. Brown	Teacher	10 years—Grade 7	No kids—married—Caucasian
Ms. Red	Teacher	10 years—Grade 3	2 young children—married—Caucasian
Ms. Pink	Teacher	25 years—Kindergarten	2 grown children—1 grandchild—married—mixed Caucasian and Chinese American
Ms. Orange	Teacher	4 years—Grade 6	No children—unmarried—Jewish
Mr. Grey	Teacher	6 months—Grade 8	No children—unmarried—gay
Ms. Purple	Office professional	30 years	3 teenagers—married—African American

Name	Role	Experience	Other
Mr. Black	Custodian	33 years	2 adopted children—widowed—mixed Caucasian and African American
Mr. Green	Educational assistant	10 years	1 grown child—divorced—Caucasian
Ms. White	Educational assistant	7 years	2 grown children—married—Baptist
Ms. Stripes	Parent	3 children—2 at school	Parent Council chair and weekly school volunteer—Caucasian
Ms. Dots	Parent	1 child and 2 stepchildren—all at school	New to your school—Caucasian
Ms. Checks	Parent	2 grandchildren at school	Children attended and grandchildren now attend your school—Caucasian
Mr. Pattern	Parent	2 stepchildren at school	Minister at local Anglican church—Caucasian
John	Student	Grade 6	Caucasian
Jane	Student	Grade 7	Caucasian
Tevon	Student	Grade 8	African American

Pick your team:

    Teaching staff: _____

    Nonteaching staff: _____

    Community representative: _____

    Student representative: _____

There is no right or wrong selection in this case study. There are simply choices and reflection. Reflect on how you made your choices. Did you have enough information to make an informed choice? If not, what other information would you like to have had?

SELF-REFLECTION

Ask yourself the following: What type of information do you need about the people you are considering for the team? Does their gender matter? Does their ethnicity matter? Does their marital status or sexual orientation matter? Do their religious affiliations or beliefs matter? Other?

_____

_____

_____

_____

ACTION: MAKING THE CUT—PICK YOUR SAFE SCHOOLS TEAM

Warm-Up Activity:

Start by creating a list of all of the possible team members. Develop brief biographies for each person to start to see what benefits and views each can offer to the team. Think back to what information you wished you had when you made your choices in the case study for this chapter and determine if you have enough information about your potential team members. If you don't, start to think about how you are going to find out the information you need to make good decisions.

Main Activity:

Now you begin the vetting process to narrow down the list of potential team candidates. You will need to start talking to your potential candidates to be sure that they have an honest interest in being an active team member. You can use the quick survey below or use a more informal process.

Potential Safe Schools Team Member Survey:

1. Do you think that bullying is a problem at this school? Yes No
2. Have you ever been a bully? Yes No
3. Have you ever been bullied? Yes No
4. Have you ever been a bystander? Yes No
5. Do you have any preconceived biases that might affect your ability to be on this team? Yes No
6. Do you want to be part of this Safe Schools Team? Yes No

Follow-Up Activity:

Review the survey answers and confirm that your potential team members fit with your thoughts about them. Then invite them to be part of your team.

SECTION I

Pre-Bystanderism

Personal History Primes Perceptions

FOLLOWING THE PATH BACKWARD

This book starts with following the path backward. As I mentioned in the preface, I am going back to the beginning, following the path out of the silo of education. I'm moving out of my arena of comfort and expertise into the fields of the social sciences and social economics to create a framework in which to examine bullying from a deeper level understanding.

When I think back on my personal history, I understand that I have made the mistake of starting at the finish line. I've gone to school every September of my life. School is all I really know. I've been a student, a teacher, and a principal. I have friends who work in the "real" world. They live in a world that is not broken up into 40-minute intervals, a world where bells don't signal that it's time to eat, where you can actually drink your coffee when it's warm, and where you can use the washroom anytime you want. They go to meetings and talk to adults and do "stuff" all day. My world, the world of education, is frighteningly the same as you probably remember it as a student. The bell rings and you go to class, the bell rings and you go to nutrition break, then outside to play, then inside to class again . . . repeat. The biggest change is that "recess" and "lunch" are a thing of the past and we now have two "nutrition breaks." Otherwise, schools have not changed much.

In addition, all the courses that I've taken over the past decade have revolved around school and teaching. Everything that I learned about was classroom and instruction. This is great, except that it creates the vicious cycle of someone being raised in an education setting, working in an education setting, and learning about an educational setting in isolation from the "real" world. Education makes the mistake of being very isolated from other areas. Teachers become subject specialists and go from the narrowness of undergraduate university classes to teacher's college to their classrooms. Each step of their journey locks them further into the silo of education and removes them more from other ideas. I think this happens in all fields to some extent. I would think that a fish geneticist, for example, has to focus specifically on the world of aquaculture to be successful, but unlike in education, every other person the fish geneticist meets is not another fish geneticist. As educators, every person you meet can talk "school" to us, either from their own experiences or those of their children. Add to that the sheer number of teachers, and in any given group of people "teacher talk" occurs. It becomes amazingly easy always to be a teacher and never to have to extend our thinking.

Not only do most teachers become friends with other teachers, but most of us have teachers in our families. Again, this makes our circle of knowledge and experience very specialized. I am no exception. I come from a family of teachers and for the longest time, as a result, swore that I would never be a teacher. In fact, while getting on the plane to go to teacher's college, I was still insisting that I was not going to be a teacher. I had watched my mom be a teacher my whole life. My grandfather worked for the board of education, my grandmother was a qualified teacher, my dad worked at the University of Guelph, my aunt is a teacher, and even one of my younger brothers is a teacher. I knew the truth. Teaching is not a 9:00–3:30 job with summers off. I knew that becoming a teacher meant homework for the rest of my life. I knew that becoming a teacher meant long hours, hard work, and little thanks. Yet, even knowing all that, I got on the plane and continued the family tradition. People become teachers for many reasons. I've sat in many job interviews where some innocent new graduate tells me in all sincerity that he or she has wanted to be a teacher since kindergarten. I generally smile politely and think the applicant is crazy. I'm sure that these new graduates are telling me the truth. I'm sure that they always wanted to be teachers. I never did, however, and I still think it's ironic that I become one and even more ironic that I am now a principal. I am a teacher for all the right reasons; I just didn't figure it out in kindergarten.

A FRIEND AND A FOE

Colleen

There are events in our lives that change us. For me, I think the most pivotal moment in my school life, and as a result my whole life, happened on the first day of school the year I went into seventh grade. That's not to say that a moment like the birth of my twins has not been life changing in unbelievable ways. It's just that without this one particular instant, I'm not sure that any of the rest of my life would have unfolded in the same way. In fact, I'm sure that it wouldn't.

I was placed in Ms. L's homeroom, and I remember looking around the room and not really knowing anyone. Waverley Drive School took in kids from the surrounding elementary schools for Grades 7 and 8, so most of the kids had not been in my Grade 6 class. We started our day with locker assignments, and that's when my moment occurred. I met Colleen. She was assigned the locker next to mine, and from that moment on we were pretty much inseparable. In fact, some 25 years later she's still one of my best friends. But it was that moment on the first day of seventh grade that effectively changed everything and allowed me to navigate the social jungle of junior high, as well as high school, with relative social ease. I was by no means popular, but thanks to that chance meeting with Colleen, I always had a group of supportive friends. Based on external appearance only, it could be assumed that Colleen would be a target for bullies. She was taller than the rest of us, already standing six feet. In addition to being taller and heavier, she also had a well-developed bust; large, bushy eyebrows; and a slightly crooked nose. You might think that she would be a target for name-calling and social isolation, but that could not have been further from the truth. Colleen was easily one of the most liked kids in the school, and no one ever mentioned her physical appearance. It wasn't a case of no one saying anything to her face but then talking behind her back, either. People genuinely liked her and wanted to be her friend.

That seemingly unimportant moment set off a series of events that allowed me to be successful not only in junior high and high school but throughout my life. Meeting Colleen resulted in my having positive experiences in the crucial preteen and teen years. I was happy to go to school and didn't experience social barriers to my learning. I had people to sit with at lunch and hang out with in the hallways. Meeting Colleen gave me the social safety to be myself and develop the self-confidence that no amount of support from my parents could have created. Our friendship allowed me to access the education I needed to be successful as an adult. Having Colleen as a friend is still the cornerstone of many of the successes in my life, and it all started with a random assignment of a locker in Grade 7.

Chris

While the start of my friendship with Colleen was a pivotal positive moment, my interactions with Chris were not. Calling him my nemesis would probably be an overstatement since I'm certain that he doesn't even remember me, yet I remember him clearly. I met Chris when I was in kindergarten. That was way back when *Star Wars* was popular the first time round, and my prize possession at the time was a Luke Skywalker action figure with a retractable light saber. I proudly brought my action figure to school one day, and Chris took it. I can remember, as if it were yesterday, standing in the hallway with Mme. T and hearing her say she believed his story that it was his doll. She believed him because according to her, boys had Luke Skywalker dolls while I would have a princess Leia figurine. He smirked as he walked away, and I never got my doll back. As an adult looking back, I can understand that it was just a doll and not really a big deal in the grand scheme of life. However, that moment set up a power dynamic that existed between the two us until the end of high school. It was also the moment I decided that I hated Mme. T and school.

Thankfully, the next year I didn't have her as a teacher, but Chris continued to be my foe. Every Monday after school I had to walk to piano lessons. It was a fairly long walk, but I usually had just enough time to make it—until Chris started waiting for me, taking my books away, and throwing them into the bushes. I would retrieve them and run as fast as I could to my piano teacher's house. There I would proceed to get chastised for not taking better care of my books. It wasn't long before I was walking the long way to my piano lessons. But I couldn't win. If I went the short way, Chris took my books; if I went the long way, I was late for my lessons and in trouble for that. Soon I was sprinting from school, as fast as I could, so that I could go the long way, avoid Chris, and make it to piano lessons on time. By the time I was in Grade 2, I had become a very fast runner thanks to my weekly sprints. I changed schools in Grade 3 and had a reprieve from Chris for years. This is not to say that everyone else that I met throughout my school years was a nice and kind person. There were other people with whom I did not get along, but no one was constant negative force in my life the way Chris had been.

If my interactions with Chris had ended in Grade 2, then calling him my nemesis would definitely be an overstatement. However, Chris reappeared in my life in high school. I'm certain he didn't know that I was the same person that he had tormented all those years ago. I know he didn't put together the Grade 9 girl that was in the hallways with the little kid whose toy he'd taken or whose piano books he'd thrown into the bushes. In fact, he didn't even know my name. He took to calling me Sharona and singing the song "My Sharona" every time I walked by. As annoying as he was, Colleen managed to laugh him off, which allowed me to do the same. In a weird way, her laughing at his singing and teasing actually gave me an odd sort of popularity. He would sing out from the front foyer, where all the senior boys and football players hung out. It wasn't long before all the popular guys knew me and acknowledged I was alive. They thought my name was Sharona, but for a "minor niner," being known by the seniors, in any form, was actually a plus. Chris continued to be a thorn in my side and would do his best to embarrass me at every opportunity, but it never worked thanks to the fact that he never managed to embarrass Colleen. She would laugh it off, and as a result no one went along with him. The luck of having a friend like Colleen meant that my foe was unable to ruin my educational experience.

As administrators and educational professionals, we have all been primed in our perceptions of bullying via our own friends and foes. Hopefully we all have at least one Colleen in our lives and very few Chrises. The way we have been primed throughout our lives means we tend to see situations through our own stereotypes or biases. Our analysis of an incident and the people involved is subjective due to our unconscious beliefs.

SELF-REFLECTION
Think of your own story. Who has primed your understanding of bullying?
Friend:
Foe:

Just as there are two sides to every story, there are two sides to priming. We need to consider our own priming and the positives and negatives that come with it, as well as the potential to use priming as a tool to motivate educators to take action.

> A principal can influence the staff's attitudes and behavior by putting anti-bullying work in the school's official agenda, initiating plenary meetings with staff and parents, and providing clear guidelines about the organization of the supervisory system during break periods. It is important that the principal allocate time and financial resources to such activities. (Olweus, 2004, p. 32)

SELF-REFLECTION

Reflect on what you can do in your school to prime your staff so that they are focused on their role in bullying episodes.

Daily:

_____

_____

Monthly:

_____

_____

THE PRIMING PROBLEM

The priming problem is a complicated one. While we can use priming to change the perceptions educational professionals have about bullying, we first must understand how our preconceived beliefs affect our ability to intervene in bullying episodes. In 2005 I began to think about bullying in earnest, and in 2006 I chose the topic as the major focus of my research for my Master of Education. I completed a study that examined the structural and attitudinal barriers that keep educational professionals in the role of bystander. My study arose from the statistics in research by Craig, Pepler, and Atlas (2000). Theirs was one of the first studies to frame educational professionals as bystanders, whether consciously or subconsciously. Overall, the purpose of my study was to examine how underlying attitudes and beliefs influence the role educational professionals play in bullying episodes at school. When the intervention cycle is analyzed, we can see that priming becomes a roadblock at the very first part of the decision-making process. The first step is noticing that something unusual or inappropriate is going on (Huston, Ruggiero, Conner, & Geis, 1981). If we cannot see beyond our own priming, we will only be able to see problems in situations that directly reflect our own experiences.

When I asked educational professionals which of the types of bullying are a problem in their schools, I found that they are generally good at identifying the "classic" types of bullying. As you can see from Table 2.1, which summarizes the results of my research, the majority of respondents noted physical, verbal, social, and reactive-victim bullying as problems. However, the majority chose "agree" rather than "strongly agree" as their preferred response. All other forms of bullying—racial, sexual, homophobic, religious-based, gender-based, and class-based—were not seen a problem by the majority of adults in the school buildings. When asked to respond to the statement "There is a high degree of bullying at your school," almost half of respondents (46.6%) disagreed, and a majority (68.1%) felt that the time and resources dedicated to antibullying were insufficient to deal with the problem. The most telling part of the data is that for all the statement options given, a percentage of respondents, ranging from 2.8 percent to 30 percent, answered, "I don't know." It is this lack of awareness that halts their entrance into the cycle of intervention. If educational professionals are unaware of the types of bullying that occur in their schools, they are unable to intervene in the situations that arise and will therefore remain in the role of bystander.

| **Table 2.1** | Summary of Results of Author Research Conducted in 2008: Responses to Question 2 |

Based on your personal experience and perspective, indicate the extent to which you agree or disagree with each of the following statements.					
	Strongly Disagree	**Disagree**	**Agree**	**Strongly Agree**	**Don't Know**
Physical bullying is a serious problem among students at your school.	1.7%	41.3%	**42.5%**	9.5%	5.0%
Verbal bullying is a serious problem among students at your school.	1.1%	17.8%	**45.0%**	31.1%	5.0%
Social bullying is a serious problem among students at your school.	2.2%	23.9%	**49.4%**	17.8%	6.7%
Cyber bullying is a serious problem among students at your school.	2.8%	**33.3%**	25.0%	8.9%	30.0%
Racial bullying is a serious problem among students at your school.	10.6%	**68.3%**	8.9%	0.6%	11.7%
Sexual bullying is a serious problem among students at your school.	4.4%	**45.0%**	22.8%	3.3%	24.4%
Homophobic bullying is a serious problem among students at your school.	4.4%	**41.7%**	25.6%	10.0%	18.3%
Religious-based bullying is a serious problem among students at your school.	15.0%	**63.9%**	3.3%	1.1%	16.7%
Gender-based bullying is a serious problem among students at your school.	3.4%	**48.0%**	32.2%	5.1%	11.3%
Reactive-victim-based bullying is a serious problem among students at your school.	1.7%	28.3%	**48.9%**	6.1%	15.0%

(Continued)

(Continued)

	Strongly Disagree	Disagree	Agree	Strongly Agree	Don't Know
Class-based bullying is a serious problem among students at your school.	4.4%	**41.1%**	34.4%	9.4%	10.6%
There is a high degree of bullying at your school.	2.8%	**42.8%**	39.9%	9.6%	3.9%
Antibullying education is one of the highest priorities in your school.	3.9%	**45.6%**	41.1%	6.7%	2.8%
Relative to other priorities, antibullying receives a substantial time and resource commitment.	5.0%	**43.3%**	42.2%	5.0%	4.4%
The amount of time and resources dedicated to bullying prevention is sufficient to effectively deal with bullying at your school.	11.7%	**56.4%**	25.1%	3.9%	2.8%

I also asked how often students report various types of bullying to educational professionals in their schools. The question has a 5-point Likert scale design with answers ranging from *never* to *always*.

As you can see from Table 2.2, verbal and social bullying are reported frequently, while physical, gender-based, and reactive-victim bullying are reported sometimes. Racial, sexual, and homophobic bullying are only reported rarely, and cyber and religious-based bullying are never reported to the majority of educational adults. The awareness of the educational professional of bullying episodes often depends on the information they receive from students. When students do not report the bullying behaviors, it becomes difficult for the educational professionals to enter into step 1 of the cycle and notice that inappropriate behaviors are occurring.

I then pushed further and asked the respondents to indicate all the reasons they would not intervene in a bullying situation. Across all employee groups, the overwhelmingly most popular response (81.9%) was "I was not aware of the situation" (see Table 3.3 in Chapter 3). While this result was concerning, I was excited to see it. What became evident is that a general lack of awareness exists with regard to what is occurring in schools on a daily basis and where these incidents physically occur.

Table 2.2	Summary of Results of Author Research Conducted in 2008: Responses to Question 3

Based on your personal experience and perspective, indicate how often the various kinds of bullying are brought to your attention.

	Never	Rarely	Sometimes	Frequently	Always
Physical bullying	1.7%	10.6%	**44.7%**	37.4%	5.6%
Verbal bullying	1.7%	3.3%	30.0%	**56.1%**	8.9%
Social bullying	3.3%	15.0%	38.3%	**41.7%**	1.7%
Cyber bullying	**38.9%**	32.2%	23.9%	4.4%	0.6%
Racial bullying	34.1%	**50.3%**	14.0%	1.7%	0.0%
Sexual bullying	25.7%	**46.4%**	24.0%	3.9%	0.0%
Homophobic bullying	25.0%	**38.3%**	26.7%	8.9%	1.1%
Religious-based bullying	**54.2%**	41.3%	3.9%	0.6%	0.0%
Gender-based bullying	13.3%	36.1%	**42.2%**	8.3%	0.0%
Reactive-victim bullying	6.8%	22.0%	**44.6%**	24.3%	2.3%

It is this lack of knowledge that prevents the intervention of educational professionals in bullying episodes, as it stalls the decision-making process before it even begins; they cannot intervene because they do not perceive that anything is happening. Lack of awareness, however, is changeable. Because the chief reason for inaction is changeable, the very thing that causes much of our inaction, priming, can become the very thing that motivates us to act. If a lack of awareness of school-bullying situations renders educational professionals unconsciously incompetent to intervene and break the cycle of bullying, then through awareness we can impact the cycle of inaction.

Priming can also be an attitudinal roadblock for educators in the pre-bystanderism section of the Continuum to Action. The bystander must decide if help is needed or if the situation can resolve itself. Several sections of the survey addressed educators' underlying beliefs regarding bullying. These underlying beliefs influence educational professionals' perception of whether or not help is warranted in the situation. If they determine that the victim does not require support, they will be unable to move from the role of bystander and instead remain stuck in the inaction section of the continuum.

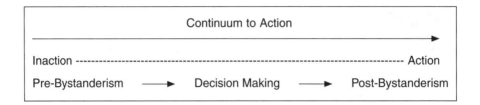

To understand better how our priming affects our beliefs, I provided the respondents with 18 statements with which to agree or disagree, some being myths and others truths. Table 2.3 summarizes the responses to each statement.

Statements such as "Bullying is just a normal part of growing up" and "Bullying toughens you up" have been proven to be untrue. However, 10.6 percent of respondents agreed or strongly agreed that bullying is a normal part of growing up. When these educational professionals see or hear accounts of bullying, their internal bias may influence their ability to deal with the situation without prejudice or at all. When those educational professionals observe a bullying incident and determine it to be normal, they are less likely to say or do anything about it and will remain bystanders.

Some statements can be classed as bullying truths, such as "Everyone is capable of bullying," yet 14.4 percent of respondents disagreed or strongly disagreed with the statement. Some statements were not clearly truths or myths. For example, statements such as "Violence on television creates violent children" have become a widely held belief, and indeed 65.9 percent of respondents either agreed or strongly agreed with the statement. Freedman, a professor at the University of Toronto, conceded that while some correlations exist between watching violent television and aggressive behaviors, he believed that no causal effect is involved. He also highlighted that violent crime rates have been declining over the past 15 years, which is contrary to the theory that an increase in violent media causes more social aggression. Furthermore, a lot of people watch violent television, but very few are violent. The same is true within a school. All the students are potentially exposed to the same television shows and video games, yet only a few become bullies (Freedman, 2001).

While each of the 18 statements can be argued as being either a truth or a myth or somewhere in between, the most interesting part of the data as it relates to the educational professional as a bystander is that regardless of the statement, a portion of the surveyed population always responded in each of the four categories. This suggests that in any given situation, educational professionals may not deem that help is necessary, as a result of their internal beliefs, and therefore will not intervene.

Table 2.3	Summary of Results of Author Research Conducted in 2008: Responses to Question 1

Read the following statements and indicate whether you strongly agree, agree, disagree, or strongly disagree.

Statement	Strongly Agree	Agree	Disagree	Strongly Disagree
Bullying is just a normal part of growing up.	0.5%	10.1%	**54.8%**	34.4%
Boys bully more than girls.	0.0%	3.9%	**58.4%**	37.6%
Victims should simply ignore the bully.	1.1%	9.5%	**60.9%**	28.5%
Bullying toughens you up.	0.5%	2.8%	40.3%	**56.3%**
Bullies have low self-esteem.	21.9%	**52.0%**	22.3%	3.9%
Victims usually bring the trouble on themselves.	0.0%	3.9%	**61.7%**	34.4%
Bullies are just having fun. They don't mean to hurt anyone.	0.6%	0.0%	36.5%	**63.0%**
If the victims improved their social skills they wouldn't be bullied.	0.0%	16.9%	**55.6%**	27.5%
Everyone is capable of bullying.	27.1%	**58.6%**	11.6%	2.8%
Children who are bullied grow up to be stronger and more self-reliant.	0.0%	1.1%	**50.8%**	48.0%
Violence on TV creates violent children.	12.8%	**53.1%**	32.4%	2.2%
Victims are too sensitive.	0.6%	0.6%	**50.6%**	48.3%
Bullies are secure people.	1.1%	5.1%	**52.5%**	41.2%
Large class sizes are responsible for the increase in bullying.	2.2%	23.3%	**61.7%**	12.8%
Physical bullying is more hurtful than verbal bullying.	0.0%	1.1%	**51.9%**	47.0%
Victims can stop the bully if they fight back.	0.0%	13.9%	**67.8%**	18.3%
Bullies don't have any friends.	1.1%	8.3%	**73.3%**	17.2%
Bullies come from dysfunctional families.	1.1%	21.3%	**65.1%**	12.4%

BROADENING THE PATH

Sometimes following the path backward allows you to move your thinking off the beaten path and onto not just a road but a multilane highway. As I followed my own path backward and began to think deeply about my own story of bullying and who had shaped my beliefs, I realized just how many on- and off-ramps my highway actually had. At first I focused on my parents and my family, who were and are huge influencers on who I am and how my life continues to unfold. However, it was through what Judy Rich Harris, author of *The Nurture Assumption* (1998), pointed out about how our peers influence our behaviors in social settings in order to create acceptance that I really understood the profound importance of my childhood friends and foes. It was through going further in my thinking about the very social setting of schools that I began to understand the current influences of my fellow educators and their beliefs and actions and the students with whom I have interacted during my career. The comments from colleagues that I would hear every now and then and would make me stop and catch my breath were all part of the prethinking that led to my formal research work. It was the table talk in the staffrooms, said with pride, about walking slowly to stop the fight so that the kids could get one more punch in or the comments about a student deserving it that tugged at my mind. The more I thought, the more uncomfortable I felt as I found myself realizing that I was, through my lack of speaking up, in the bystander category too. That thinking came back into my conscious mind during the Ontario Principals' Council presentation, whose data enraged me. There I heard that Craig et al. (2000) had discovered that teachers only intervened in 14 percent of classroom bullying episodes and 4 percent of playground episodes. This both angered me and offended my integrity. My rage was a good defense against the discomfort of the things I knew to be true. I focused and learned a lot. When I moved my focus out of the silos of education, I learned even more. When I began to think in the realm of the larger social sciences or social economics and move out of the limits of education, my understanding of bullying and bystanders really began to develop.

As educational professionals, we need to acknowledge that we are human and can only do our best. However, it is also an integral part of our duty to do better once we know better. Broadening our understanding of our own stories and the stories of our colleagues allows us to make more conscious and informed choices. Through realizing what beliefs are true and which ones lead us to inaction, we can remove the attitudinal barriers that cause us to remain bystanders. The educational professionals on your staff are no different. Their personal experiences with bullying will affect what situations they are aware of and how they deal with situations once they are aware of them.

It is important for educational professionals to be reflective with regard to their own attitudes toward, perceptions of, and beliefs about bullying. It is only through exploring our internal dialogues that we can move beyond our prejudices and begin to become active and unbiased interveners.

CASE STUDY: CAN YOU SPOT THE BULLY?

Read the description of the students below and decide whether or not each is a bully. Go with you first instincts—doing so will help you determine what your primed perspective is—and don't peek ahead to the answers.

Student 1: Miranda is a Grade 5 girl with beautiful curly blond hair and striking blue eyes. She sings in the junior choir and is a B+ student. She is the youngest in her family and has two older sisters in high school.

Student 2: David is also in Grade 5. He is the oldest of his siblings. He has two younger siblings in the school, a younger half sister who is still a toddler, and two other half sisters who attend a different school. He and his two brothers have been in foster care for the past two years, and before that he was raised by his unmarried, meth-addicted mother.

Student 3: Evan is in Grade 1. He is a C student. Evan is the only child in his family. His mom stays at home, and his dad works at the local factory.

Student 4: Kerri Anne is in Grade 4. She is the youngest in her family and has an older brother in Grade 7 at the junior high school. Kerri Anne has an Individual Educational Plan and struggles academically. Her mom recently remarried, so Kerri Anne now has a new stepfather, as well as two younger stepsiblings.

How many of the four students in the case study did you label as a bully? I'll give you a hint: three of the four students described above are based on students who have exhibited bullying behaviors. Look at your answers again. Do you want to change them before you read on for the answers?

Answers:

Student 1: Bully   Student 2: Not a bully   Student 3: Bully   Student 4: Bully

Where you right? Now try to match the type of bullying each of the case students exhibited with their descriptions. Who is the sexual bully? Who is the physical bully? Who is the exclusionary bully?

Answers:

Student 1: Sexual bully   Student 3: Physical bully   Student 4: Exclusionary bully

Were you right? If so, what lead you to your conclusions? If you were wrong, what in your primed belief system and primed experiences led you to different answers?

ACTION: FACT OR MYTH?

Warm-Up Activity:

Divide your staff into groups and have them brainstorm different statements they have heard with regard to bullying. They can think of truths or myths. Once each group has thought of three statements, it should be prepared to share them with the entire staff and say whether or not the statements are fact or fiction.

Variation: Once the group has made its statement, have the rest of the staff indicate by a show of hands whether they believe the statement to be fact or fiction.

Main Activity:

Four Corners: Label the four corners of your meeting room as *strongly agree, agree, disagree,* and *strongly disagree*. Explain to your staff that they need to move to the appropriate sign based on their opinions of the statements on the next page. You will also want to create a "pass" zone somewhere in the room where staff members can go if they choose to pass on responding to some of the statements.

Some of the statements are believed to be truths, and some are believed to be myths. Emphasize to your staff that there are no "right" or "wrong" answers. After you have read the statements with your staff and they have moved into one of the four corners, you may wish to choose from the following options:

1. Have volunteers defend their choice to those with a differing opinion.

2. Tally the number of staff in each corner and compare your results to the results found in the research.

3. Have staff pick different statements and research them on the Internet to try to determine which ones are truths and which are myths.

Exit Activity:

Have staff complete a feedback sheet indicating one statement that they now feel differently about after the discussion.

Follow-Up Activity:

Examine the beliefs of the staff with regard to the statements below to determine in what areas they need more education. If staff responses are split or spread out, have the Safe Schools Team examine the statement and bring back more information to the staff to educate them around either the "fact" or "myth." This information can be shared through weekly memos, staff notices, or a future meeting.

Truth or Myth Statements

Bullying is just a normal part of growing up.

Boys bully more than girls.

Victims should simply ignore the bully.

Bullying toughens you up.

Bullies have low self-esteem.

Victims usually bring the trouble on themselves.

Bullies are just having fun. They don't mean to hurt anyone.

If the victims improved their social skills, they wouldn't be bullied.

Everyone is capable of bullying.

Children who are bullied grow up to be stronger and more self-reliant.

Violence on TV creates violent children.

Victims are too sensitive.

Bullies are secure people.

Large class sizes are responsible for the increase in bullying.

Physical bullying is more hurtful than verbal bullying.

Victims can stop the bully if they fight back.

Bullies don't have any friends.

Bullies come from dysfunctional families.

Good Intentions Can Get Lost

THE KITTY GENOVESE STORY

The story of Kitty Genovese was one of my first "Aha!" moments when thinking about bystanders in bullying situations. When I heard about the story, it was the first time that I really began to understand that the problem of bystanders is not exclusive to schools or exclusive to children. Those two realizations became the catalyst for my seeking to understand the complexity and vastness of bystanderism.

Kitty Genovese was the product of the classic American dream. She was the eldest daughter of a middle-class Italian American family. When Kitty was 19, her mother witnessed a murder, so her family moved from Brooklyn to the suburbs of Connecticut. Kitty, however, chose to stay in New York City. She worked and lived in the city for the next nine years until she was stabbed to death on the night of March 13, 1964.

Kitty was coming home late from her job as a bar manager when she had the fatal misfortune of being seen by Winston Mosley in the parking lot of her apartment building. Mosley, who was later diagnosed as a necrophiliac, quickly overpowered Kitty and stabbed her twice in the back. Kitty screamed and fought back, but her cries fell on deaf ears. The *New York Times* reported that there were 38 witnesses to this attack. While this was later proven to be an exaggeration, dozens of people did hear her cries, including her explicit cries of "Oh my God, he stabbed me!" and "Help me!" and did nothing. Kitty made so much noise and screamed for help with such force that Mosley actually gave up at one point in the attack and left the scene of the crime. He drove away and left Kitty for ten minutes before returning and systematically searching for her again. He found her, barely conscious, outside the locked door of her apartment building and proceeded to rape and to kill her. During the 30 minutes that Kitty fought for her life, none of her neighbors intervened. One man yelled out the window to leave her alone, but no one called the police until ten minutes after the final attack was over. The police arrived quickly once notified, but it was too late; Kitty died of her injuries en route to the hospital.

This case became the benchmark example of the bystander effect and raised the question of how so many people could hear a brutal murder taking place and not help. For my part, I thought about this case on many levels. The first and most basic level was a personal one. As a female who has walked alone at various hours of the night in many major cities of the world, New York included, I was stunned by the revelation that if I were screaming for my life, there was a good chance that no one would help. It had never occurred to me that other human beings could hear someone in need and do nothing. I had never thought that diffusion of responsibility could have such a deadly outcome. Diffusion of responsibility is the social phenomenon seen when a large group shares responsibility for something without anyone having an explicit role. No one takes action, as everyone in the large group thinks someone else will do something. In the case of Kitty Genovese, all the witnesses thought that someone else would call for help or do something, and as a result no one did anything until it was too late. I then began to consider how this phenomenon manifests in schools, creating bystanders to bullying.

Altruistic inertia in our schools is paralyzing. When education professionals were asked to indicate the reasons that they did not intervene in bullying episodes, the most popular answer was lack of awareness, but the second most popular response was "I told the students to talk to the teacher on duty." Of respondents, 22.1 percent not only assumed a passive role due to diffusion of responsibility but purposefully passed the responsibility to another person (see Table 3.1). The data become much more interesting when the educational professionals were asked why they think others do not intervene when witnessing bullying behaviors. Study the data shared in Table 3.2: think about the data in terms of ownership of actions, and think of the responses in terms of the ability of the respondent to pass responsibility on to others. Over half of the respondents thought that their colleagues "didn't want to get involved," "didn't have time because the bell rang," or "didn't respond because they weren't the teacher on duty," and just less that half felt their colleagues didn't intervene because "the students weren't in their class."

Table 3.1	Summary of Results of Author Research Conducted in 2008: Responses to Question 4

Indicate all the reasons you would not intervene in a bullying situation. (Check all that apply.)	
The bell rang and I didn't have time.	9.4%
I didn't want to get involved.	1.3%
I didn't know what to do or whom to talk to.	5.4%
I thought if I intervened I would not be supported.	12.1%
I was physically afraid to become involved.	10.1%
The person being bullied deserved it. They brought it on themselves.	0.0%
It was just teasing, not bullying.	5.4%
I didn't want to make things worse.	6.0%
I wasn't the person on duty.	5.4%
The students involved were not in my class.	0.0%
It wouldn't have made a difference.	3.4%
The bullying was happening off property.	12.8%
I was not aware of the situation.	**81.9%**
I'm not the parent. It's their job.	0.0%
The students need to be able to resolve problems on their own.	6.7%
It was just horseplay and fooling around.	12.8%
The students are friends.	6.0%
The students are just jockeying for social position.	0.0%
I can't make the kids play together and be friends.	12.8%
I told the students to talk to the teacher on duty.	22.1%

SELF-REFLECTION

Think about your school and your staff. Does diffusion of responsibility exist in your building? How would you know?

_____

_____

_____

Table 3.2	Summary of Results of Author Research Conducted in 2008: Responses to Question 8

What reason(s) do you think other educational professionals (administrators, office professionals, custodians, educational assistants, and teachers) have for not intervening when witnessing bullying behaviors? (Check all that apply.)	
They didn't want to get involved.	51.8%
They didn't know what to do or whom to talk to.	31.8%
They thought they would not be supported.	37.6%
They were physically afraid to intervene.	30.6%
They thought the person being bullied deserved it.	11.8%
It was just teasing, not bullying.	33.5%
They didn't want to make things worse.	14.1%
The bell rang and they didn't have time.	52.4%
They weren't the teacher on duty.	52.4%
The students weren't in their class.	42.4%
It wouldn't have made a difference.	20.0%
The bullying was happening off property.	46.5%
They were not aware of the situation.	**83.5%**
It wasn't their job. They weren't the parent.	20.6%
The students needed to be able to resolve problems on their own.	24.1%

GOOD SAMARITANS: THE PARABLE "FROM JERUSALEM TO JERICHO"

The idea of a good Samaritan has been interwoven into Christian story-telling for centuries. Regardless of faith or belief system, humans hold close to their hearts the idea that if they were ever in need, someone would help them. That is why the story of Kitty Genovese was so shocking and why the idea that we as educational professionals may be bystanders is so uncomfortable for us.

Even though I'd heard the phrase "good Samaritan" and had a general idea what it meant, I could not in all honesty have told you any details of the original biblical story until I looked it up. If you are already familiar with the Gospel according to Luke, then jump ahead. If not, then here is the parable, taken from the New International Version of the Bible:

In reply Jesus said: "A man was going down from Jerusalem to Jericho, when he fell into the hands of robbers. They stripped him of his clothes, beat him and went away, leaving him half dead. A priest happened to be going down the same road, and when he saw the man, he passed by on the other side. So too, a Levite, when he came to the place and saw him, passed by on the other side. But a Samaritan, as he traveled, came where the man was; and when he saw him, he took pity on him. He went to him and bandaged his wounds, pouring on oil and wine. Then he put the man on his own donkey, took him to an inn and took care of him. The next day he took out two silver coins and gave them to the innkeeper. 'Look after him,' he said, 'and when I return, I will reimburse you for any extra expense you may have.'

"Which of these three do you think was a neighbor to the man who fell into the hands of robbers?"

The expert in the law replied, "The one who had mercy on him."

Jesus told him, "Go and do likewise." (Luke 10:30–37)

The title "priest" speaks for itself. A Levite was also a person with a priestly role. Both these men might have been expected to help the beaten traveler. However, it was the Samaritan who stopped and helped the man. The fact that the person who demonstrated compassion was not who one might expect sparked the research of Darley and Latane in the late 1960s. The parable "From Jerusalem to Jericho" became the basis of one of the first experiments on the bystander effect. Darley and Latane began to investigate the phenomenon in1968, four years after the death of Kitty Genovese gave birth to the initial idea of bystander-ism. They posed the question, Just how likely are we, as human beings, to take care of each other? What motivates some people to stop and help and others to pass by?

Darley and Latane (1973) decided to focus their research on a sample group whom most people would assume would stop and try to help a person in distress. Darley and Latane recruited students from the Princeton Theological Seminary to participate in a study that examined religious education and vocations and focused on three hypotheses:

1. People who think religious, "helping" thoughts would be no more likely than others to offer assistance.

2. People in a hurry will be less likely to offer aid than others.

3. People who enjoy the benefits religiosity bestows, such as priests, will be less likely to help than those who value religion for its own sake or are searching for meaning in life.

Darley and Latane (1973) started their experiment by having the students complete a personality questionnaire about their religion. They then had the students walk from one building on campus to another. En route the students would encounter a man slumped in an alleyway. Darley and Latane included several variables in their experiment. The subjects had been asked to prepare a short talk on one of two topics, either seminary jobs in general or the story of the good Samaritan. At this point I think most of us are thinking the same thing: *It's obvious. Those subjects speaking on the topic of the good Samaritan will stop, and those speaking about the seminary in general will not.* Darley and Latane layered hypothesis 2 over hypothesis 1 by varying the time frame the subjects were given to get from the first building to the second. Some subjects were given low-hurry, some intermediate-hurry, and some high-hurry instructions.

1. Low-hurry. The participant was told there was still some time left before the presentation but he might as well head over.

2. Intermediate-hurry. The participant was told the audience was ready for him so he should leave right away.

3. High-hurry. The participant was informed he was late and that the audience had been expecting him for a few minutes so he had better hurry.

The man in the alleyway between the two buildings moaned and coughed twice as each subject passed. The subjects were scored on a 5-point Likert scale of helping ranging from failing to notice the victim as being in need to refusing the leave the victim or insisting on taking him somewhere. Finally the experiment was completed after the subjects arrived at the second site, gave their talks, and answered a helping behavior questionnaire.

The researchers were keenly interested in whether the participants would stop and help the man. Several interesting observations surfaced from this experiment. First, planning to give a talk on the good Samaritan had no impact whatsoever on respondents' helping behavior. In other words, even though these "primed" individuals were about to describe the importance of helping others to a large audience, they did not respond to the needs of this planted victim.

The second finding, and the most relevant to school bullying, is that time pressure was the only factor that affected responses. More specifically, 63 percent of participants in the low-hurry condition offered help to the victim, while 45 percent of participants in the intermediate condition responded in this way and only 10 percent of people in the high-hurry group stopped to help. In fact, the researchers noted, "On several occasions, a seminary student going to give his talk on the parable of the good Samaritan *literally stepped over the victim* [emphasis added] as he hurried on his way" (Darley & Latane, 1973, p. 107). The researchers reasoned as follows:

> It is difficult not to conclude from this that the frequently cited explanation that ethics becomes a luxury as the speed of our daily lives increases is at least an accurate description. (p. 107)

Table 3.1 shows the data collected when educational professionals were asked to indicate their own reasons for nonintervention, and Table 3.2 shows the data from their "revealed" answers when they were asked to respond with their perceived beliefs of their colleagues. Their responses relate directly to the findings of Darley and Latane. Of respondents, 51.8 percent felt that their colleagues "didn't want to get involved." Again, over 50 percent of respondents indicated that not having time because the bell rang was a factor in their colleagues remaining in the role of bystander. Statements such as "They weren't the teacher on duty and it's not their job" were seen as plausible. The school data support the idea that time is a main motivating factor for active involvement in bullying scenarios. Thus, as the pressure from the many expectations of educators continues to build and educational professionals experience increased job stress, their ability to see intervention in bullying as their own responsibility becomes less and less.

SELF-REFLECTION

It is important as educators to think about why the parable and the experiment discussed here are important in an educational setting. What correlations can be made between the seminary students and educators?

_____

_____

_____

How does the idea of hurriedness fit into the school day and the overall increasing pace of life?

_____

_____

A Modern Twist

Technology puts a modern twist on the idea of bystanderism. The bystanders in the Kitty Genovese case did not call the police but instead listened by their windows. In the parable experiment, most of the students did not stop because they were in a hurry. How would our modern technology affect these two scenarios? Cell phones of some kind are now carried by almost everyone, and even the cheapest cell phones have built-in cameras and video recorders. Do you think that ease of access to our own phones in our pockets, purses, or backpacks would increase our ability to help someone or increase our tendency to be a bystander?

I think most people would assume that having easy access to mobile phones, which we could use while moving to a safe location, would increase our tendency to intervene. Being able to call 911 rather than having to know the phone number for help should also increase our ability to help. Thus, modern technology should remove barriers to inaction. However, it also increases the diffusion of responsibility. Since everyone has a phone, everyone could be responsible; as a result, it becomes easier to assume that someone else will call for help. Modern technology has also provided society with another level of bystanderism that goes beyond simply not intervening to a form of voyeurism. Cell phone videos of physical assaults, sexual assaults, verbal assaults, and all types of negative activities flood the Internet on a daily basis. Beyond not helping, bystanders are now watching as entertainment.

THE BYSTANDER EFFECT: WHAT AFFECTS THE BYSTANDER?

While bullies are often created at home, victims are most often created at school (Olweus, 1993), and by extension so too are bystanders. "Teachers' attitudes, behaviors, and routines," Olweus said, "play a large role in the prevalence of bullying behavior" (Olweus as cited in Starr, 2000). He examined this concept through the lens of teachers educating students to change behaviors, and he extended this idea toward the action end of the continuum, educating teachers about their power as part of the bullying dynamic rather as merely external observers. "Bullying is a problem that schools can—and must—control" (Olweus, Limber, & Mihalic, 1999, p. 17).

Studies by Pepler and Craig (2000) have likewise repositioned the teacher from the role of external factor to that of bystander, incorporating educators into a tridactic paradigm of bullying. This internalization of the bullying triad allows educators to understand the power of their actions, moving them from being part of the problem to a crucial part of the solution. Observational studies have demonstrated that in 86 percent of classroom bullying episodes and in 96 percent of schoolyard incidents, the adults present did not intervene, instead assuming the role of bystander (Pepler & Craig).

Bullying changes all students, in some way or another, both in the short term and throughout their educational careers. Grades of students involved in the bullying triad appear to decline, and aspirations disintegrate. According to a study conducted by the National Association of School Psychologists (2001), approximately 160,000 students miss school every day due to the fear of being bullied. Apart from the academic deterioration of students, there appear to be social and emotional repercussions, which range from mild to severe (Banks, 1997). The bullied can often suffer from high levels of anxiety and emotional distress (Coloroso, 2003). They might also have a lower self-concept and often exhibit psychosomatic health problems. Moreover, the bullied can experience social isolation and lose friends as others try to avoid becoming victims by association (Coloroso). The victim then experiences loneliness due to difficulty making social and emotional adjustments, difficulty making friends, and poor relationships with peers (Coloroso). According to research by Banks, the bullied are four to five times more likely to consider suicide than the nonbullied.

It is also reported that the psychological effects do not stop at the end of the day, the end of the school year, or the end of high school (Hoover & Oliver, 1996). In a study of over 100,000 students from 25 countries, both victims of bullying and bullies themselves were found to suffer serious long-term effects, including poorer social, emotional, and physical health compared to those not involved in bullying. These problems were also found to continue into adolescence and adulthood (Nansel et al., 2004). The research concludes that both bullies and the bullied are at risk of developing psychosocial and psychiatric problems that may continue into adulthood (Nansel et al., 2001; Olweus, 1993). Higher levels of depression and lower self-esteem are reported to persist in studies of adults who experienced bullying in their childhoods (Weinhold & Weinhold, 1998).

More recently the psychological ramifications for the bystander, whether that bystander is a child or an adult, are also becoming better understood. Hoel, Sparks, and Cooper (2001) determined that there is a cost—physical, psychological, and financial—to stress and violence in the workplace. According to Hoel and his associates, educational professionals who are bystanders to bullying suffer negative repercussions such as absenteeism and reduced productivity, and their organizations suffer replacement and retirement costs. In addition, long-term traumatic effects may cause physical and mental impairment. Thus, bullying, as well as its resulting climate of fear, has both an economic and social cost.

General job stress has increasingly become accepted as being part of the workplace experience (Cox, Griffiths, & Rial-González, 2000), and education is no exception. Educational professionals now experience stress that is no longer related to the content they teach but arises from the social dynamics in schools. This stress, in addition to the stress of being a bystander, is creating not only an economic cost for education but an emotional one (International Labour Organization, 2003). The Canadian Public Health Association, in its Safe School Study (2004), likewise suggested that we need to look at bullying as a public health issue.

The emotional and public health issues associated with being a bystander also translate into economic consequences. Increased absenteeism, in both the short and long term, costs school boards money. The negative school climate that bullying creates directly impacts operating costs, as educational employees require more sick days, medical treatment, and, in some cases, long-term benefits and social assistance (International Labour Organization, 2003). Highly stressed teachers have a negative impact on student learning, as they can feel overwhelmed and therefore withdraw from their work and their students (Hoel et al., 2001). The increase in stress can lead to increased rates of absenteeism and, in extreme cases, severe mental health problems and suicides (Cox et al., 2000).

ARE EDUCATIONAL PROFESSIONALS GOOD SAMARITANS?

Are educational professionals good Samaritans? Well, maybe. In theory I think we would all like to believe that if a teacher, rushing to class, saw a student lying nearly dead at the side of the hallway, the teacher would stop and do whatever possible to help. However, when just over 10 percent of respondents suggest that their colleagues would not intervene because the victim deserved it, the question becomes harder to answer. It becomes harder still when the wounds are not as visible as cuts or bruises, which we can't imagine an educational professional ignoring. Would the internal wounds of verbal and social bullying be enough to make an educational professional stop? Would the educator see the potentially fatal repercussions of nonviolent bullying? As the questions become more layered, the answers become less and less clear. So "maybe" might be the best answer we have at the moment.

CASE STUDY: WHAT DO YOU SEE?

Think back to the four students from our first case study. Remember Miranda, the Grade 5 student who demonstrates sexual bullying behaviors? Here is a scenario involving her.

The bell has rung to dismiss classes to go outside for the second half of nutrition break. You see Miranda walk past a boy in her class and say something casually in passing. You can't hear what she said because of the noise in the hallway, and the boy looks more confused than upset. You ask the boy what she said to him, and he responds, "I don't know. Something about zero."

Pause: Would you have noticed this interaction? Would you think that it is out of the ordinary? Would you take the time to find out why Miranda said "zero" to the boy? Has bullying occurred?

A few days later, you hear the word zero *again about another boy in the class.*

Pause: Anything yet?

By the end of the week, another female student from the class is sent to your office in tears. After trying to get to the bottom of things, you have only bits and pieces of the story, but from what you can gather, this girl wants to be friends with Miranda but isn't a "chiclet" so she's not in the club.

Pause: Review—you have heard some of the boys being called "zeros" and now a girl can't be friends with Miranda because she's not a "chiclet." Any thoughts?

You call Miranda down to your office, and of course she has no idea what you're talking about.

Pause: Now what? You're at a dead end. Do you leave it? Wait for more information? Call other students in one at a time in the hopes of getting information? Is any of this really a big deal?

The Rest of the Story: It turns out that "chiclets" is the short form code for "chicks who lick dicks," a club started by Miranda. "Zeros" are the boys in the class who are not involved, and the rest of the boys have been given scores out of ten. The club meets outside of school hours at Miranda's house, and the girls have to "earn" their way into the club. The group also has a Facebook page.

Pause: Did you see that? Now that you know, what is your next step?

ACTION: IDENTIFY HOT SPOTS

Hot spots for bullying can occur anywhere in your school. These locations are areas in which bullying occurs more frequently. Certain sites can become prime spots for bullying for various reasons, with the main ones being lack of awareness on the part of the staff and lack of staff presence. In research conducted in the Bluewater District School Board, Ontario, 81.9 percent of employees indicated that the main reason they did not intervene in bullying episodes was that they were not aware of the situation. Furthermore, when asked about the occurrence of bullying in various locations throughout their schools, a large percentage of respondents gave "I don't know" as an answer. The responses to the question "During the past month of school, with what frequency has bullying behavior occurred in the following locations?" are collated in Table 3.3.

As you can see from the statistics, there are many areas within the school where staff are unaware of whether or not bullying is occurring. Though unintentional, this lack of awareness causes us as educational professionals to be unconsciously incompetent with regard to bullying prevention.

Warm-Up Activity:

This activity should be completed individually before the staff comes together for discussion. Have your staff complete the survey regarding where different types of bullying occur in your school. Collate the responses and have them ready for discussion. The survey should be completed anonymously to generate the most honest answers.

Discussion of the collated responses will be your starting point. The most important thing to examine with your staff is what trends emerge. These will be different for every school. Your focus should be on the "I don't know" answers and trying to determine why staff is unaware of what activities occur in these locations.

Main Activity:

Ideally this activity should be completed several times per year, as the "staff-free" zones and "hot spots" will vary.

The first part of this activity will take place over a two-week period. You may want to extend or shorten the timeline depending on the size of your school and staff. Give every staff member a copy of your school map. Have staff members mark the routes that they travel throughout the day. For example, what hallways do they walk through to get from the staffroom to their classroom, or which entrance to the building do they use? Also have them mark on the map any locations where they observe or deal with

Table 3.3	Summary of Results of Author Research Conducted in 2008: Responses to Question 5

During the past month of school, with what frequency has bullying behavior occurred in the following locations?

	Rarely	Biweekly	Weekly	Daily	Don't Know
Classrooms	19.0%	13.2%	24.7%	**29.9%**	13.2%
Hallways	14.3%	14.3%	18.3%	**41.7%**	11.4%
Stairwells	20.2%	0.0%	4.3%	6.1%	**69.3%**
Entrances/exits	17.4%	9.9%	19.8%	25.0%	**27.9%**
Library	35.8%	2.9%	2.9%	6.4%	**52.0%**
Computer lab	34.7%	2.9%	2.4%	2.9%	**57.1%**
Gym	26.7%	8.5%	16.5%	8.0%	**40.3%**
Change rooms	22.8%	5.3%	9.4%	9.9%	**52.6%**
Washrooms	24.0%	10.3%	13.1%	12.0%	**40.6%**
School bus	12.4%	10.7%	10.7%	20.9%	**45.2%**
Playground	5.6%	11.3%	**19.2%**	3.1%	10.7%
To school	12.7%	5.2%	11.6%	8.1%	**62.4%**
From school	11.4%	6.9%	6.9%	10.3%	**64.6%**
Eating areas	14.2%	14.8%	18.2%	**27.3%**	25.6%
Off property/ near property	9.8%	8.0%	9.2%	8.6%	**64.4%**
During rotary*	19.1%	10.4%	13.3%	19.7%	**37.6%**
Off property/ away from property	8.0%	2.9%	5.7%	8.0%	**75.4%**

*As students move between classes

bullying during the two-week period. You can color code the different types of bullying behaviors, or you can simply use one color for travel routes and another for bullying episodes. Have your staff hand in their maps to the Safe Schools Team for the follow-up activity.

During the second part of this activity, challenge your staff to change their routines over the next two-week period. Ask your staff to travel different routes as much as possible. Have them walk different hallways

(Continued)

(Continued)

and use different entrances or stairs. Again, you can either shorten or extend the timelines as needed. All staff members should again mark off their routes on a map, as well as the location of any bullying behaviors they observe or deal with.

Main Activity Extended Options:

As a way to get a more complete view of the bullying activities in your school, you may wish to use either or both of the two extended options.

Option 1: Invite staff from another school to walk through your school and note their observations regarding where they see "staff-free" zones or bullying "hot spots."

Option 2: Select various groups of students to complete the mapping activity. Perhaps one class at each grade level or your student council members could complete the activity.

Both of these options will allow you to see your school from another perspective.

Follow-Up Activities:

The Safe Schools Team should collect and collate all of the maps. This is a large undertaking, but the information gained will be very useful. The team should examine the routes that staff take to determine whether any areas of the school are "staff-free" zones in which bullying could occur. The team should also look at where bullying episodes have been indicated to see if some locations are "hot spots" for your school.

SECTION II

Decision Making

Broken Culture: A Window of Opportunity

BROKEN WINDOWS
FROM NEW YORK TO YOUR SCHOOL

Learning about the Kitty Genovese story and the research conducted by Darley and Latane was my first "Aha!" moment, when I realized that bystanderism exists outside school. Learning about the idea of Broken Windows turned out to be my second.

That techniques used to influence society at large, through small yet tangible actions, could be effective within schools should have been obvious, but I had not given it any thought. I did understand that if you follow the rules, you don't get into trouble. Being a type-A good girl, I had always followed the rules and as a result had never dealt with the police. My behaviors had never had to be modified to fit with the expectations of society through interventions of any kind. Therefore, I had never given much thought to the philosophies behind how policing is done. Furthermore, other than reading about the Kitty Genovese story, my understanding of life in New York City was limited to one long weekend of shopping with friends and faithfully watching every episode of *Sex and the City*. I have lived a very sheltered life by most people's standards, and I am the furthest thing from a city girl you can imagine. Having been raised in the middle-class suburbs of Guelph, Ontario, my exposure to crime was limited to say the least. Even my wild party days were not all that wild and usually involved going out for dinner and drinks with my friends, who were just as middle class and suburban as I was. None of us would ever have considered not following the rules. "Rebellious" was buying our clothes at full price, so controlling crime in a city the size of New York was not at all within the scope of our imaginations.

At first, I couldn't fathom what my small, rural JK–6 school could have in common with New York City. However, the more I read about the ideas implemented in the 1990s in New York City to combat crime, the more I realized that the Broken Windows theory may provide an insight into how schools can tackle the seemingly overwhelming problem of bullying. When there is so much to do and so many things need attention, people can suffer from option paralysis and end up doing nothing. Looking at school bullying through the lens of fixing "broken windows" can make the problem seem smaller, targeted, and manageable.

The Broken Windows theory is based on the work of Kelling and Coles. In 1996 they published their book *Fixing Broken Windows: Restoring Order and Reducing Crime in Our Communities*. They combined their backgrounds in criminology and urban sociology to focus on strategies to contain or eliminate crime from urban neighborhoods. In essence, their theory is that reducing petty or low-level crimes and antisocial behaviors will deter more major crimes.

While Kelling and Coles formally published their work in the mid-1990s, the story actually started in the mid-1980s, when David Gunn of the New York City Transit Authority hired Kelling as a consultant. It was in 1985 that Gunn began the widespread implementation of the Broken Windows premise, starting by aggressively targeting graffiti on the subway system. Graffiti was definitely not a major crime and, in fact, was mostly perceived as a nuisance. However, from 1984 to 1990 the subway system was systematically cleaned car by car. The most important aspect of this time-consuming process was that once a car was reclaimed, it could not be given up. If the car was retagged by graffiti vandals, it had to be recleaned before it was put back into service. That meant many cars became part of a daily battle of being tagged and cleaned. Once the cars were cleaned, the transit authority began to target another petty crime by implementing a zero-tolerance policy on fare dodging. Mayor Giuliani approved new policing procedures that created mobile police stations; these could quickly process the crime and do on-the-spot background checks. Now something small, such as jumping the turnstiles, would result in being processed, fingerprinted, and, if the fare jumper had any previous criminal activity or outstanding warrants, arrested. Giuliani began to roll out interlocking, widespread reforms by having police strictly enforce laws about public drinking and urination, as well as "squeegee men" (people who mob cars stopped at traffic lights, threatening to slop soapy water over the windows unless they are paid off). As these reforms began, both petty and serious crime rates began to fall. In the 2001 study conducted by Kelling and Sousa, it became clear that crime trends in New York fell suddenly and significantly and continued to drop throughout the following decade.

The Broken Windows theory demonstrated such success in New York City that it was adopted by other major cities around the world. Albuquerque, New Mexico, adopted a Safe Streets program in the late 1990s that targeted its own "broken windows." Experiments in the Netherlands concluded that tackling small negative behaviors can indeed avert more serious antisocial behaviors (Keizer, Lindenberg, & Steg, 2008). Finally, research out of Massachusetts targeted "broken window" behaviors in what were considered crime hot spots. This study determined that by combining a focus on misdemeanor crimes with a concentrated locational focus, authorities could make a discernible difference in crime statistics (Braga & Bond 2008).

If we look at the Broken Windows theory through the lens of schools, we can substitute the word *bullying* for *crime* and the word *schools* for *urban neighborhoods*. By deterring low-level antisocial behavior, the educational professional can prevent major bullying.

WHAT ARE YOUR "BROKEN WINDOWS"?

Focusing on the small stuff rather than the huge umbrella of bullying can help educators move from bystander to intervener roles because the actions needed are small, tangible, and manageable. Remember that the "in the moment" section of the spectrum is comprised of the decisions that need to be made once you have determined that something unusual is going on. By mirroring the Broken Windows premise in our schools, bullying is no longer vague but instead consists of specific and noticeable behaviors to which educational professionals can respond with direct and tangible actions.

As I said, my school and New York City are worlds apart; for that matter, my school and your school probably have very limited similarities. The "broken windows" I picked in my school will not be those that you pick, but our reasons for picking them are the same. We choose them because if they are left unchanged, they will slowly erode the culture of the school. Once a culture begins to erode, opportunistic bullying begins to appear, which then further erodes the culture.

What behaviors you target are not the most important part of this activity in schools. What is important is that, as a staff, you choose your focus and all staff members and students have a shared understanding of the expectations surrounding a particular behavior. The consistency and tenacity with which you target your "broken windows" will bring success. Just as when, in

New York, the petty criminals and more the serious criminals alike realized that every time they tagged a subway car, urinated in public, or jumped their fares on the subway, they would be caught and suffer consequences, your students will figure out your expectations for behaviors in your school.

Following the Broken Windows theory serves two purposes on the Continuum to Action. The first is to create a common understanding and common ownership of clearly defined expectations for your staff. The second is to define clear expectations for your students. This seems obvious, but a school's behavior code is typically directed at students and focuses on all behaviors equally, making it difficult for staff to understand what to look for. Having too many behavioral expectations makes it easier for staff members to get stuck in inaction because they are trying to pay attention to too many things. Think back to the data shared in Tables 3.1 and 3.2: of respondents, 5.4 percent said that they don't intervene in bullying episodes because they don't know what to do, and 31.8 percent felt their peers did not intervene because they didn't know what to do. When you create a shared understanding of the "broken windows" in your school and a shared understanding of how to intervene, your staff will know what to do when they come across inappropriate behaviors. The extremely narrow focus of the Broken Windows theory effectively creates knowledge of what to do. Specifically deciding upon and then consistently targeting a particular behavior makes it easier for staff to take action.

The "broken windows" my staff and I chose to focus on may seem laughable to those of you in bigger schools with older student populations. Remember, it's not the "broken window" itself that is important; it is the consistency and tenacity with which it is targeted. As a staff we targeted movement in the hallways. The expectation was set on the first day of school that all students were to walk in a quiet, single-file line on the right-hand side of the hallway when going from one class to another or to the library, washroom, computer lab, or lunchroom. Having students walk in a straight and quiet line is manageable for staff members. They know how to enforce this rule and therefore will do so and become more confident. This type of small and tangible action makes a difference in the climate of the school and school culture. The staff feels empowered and, as a result, is more open to tackling larger problems. At the same time, the hallways become safer and quieter. It was only a matter of days before the students realized that every time they were not on the right-hand side of the hallway walking quietly, an adult would intervene and redirect them. Within a few weeks, students no longer needed reminders and began automatically walking quietly on the right-hand side of the hallway.

With one success under our belts, we chose our second "broken window." Again, remember that your "broken windows" are supposed to be seemingly petty in nature. We focused on garbage in the lunchroom. Since we are a small school, the majority of students eat together at tables in the gymnasium. This allows for supervision of a lot of students by very few staff but also means that my custodian has more work before and after each nutrition break. This extra cleaning time meant that we could not use the gym for intermural activities because the tables needed to be wiped and put away and the floors needed to be swept. As a staff, we began to have higher expectations for lunchroom cleanup. Teachers "taught" students what the expectations were, and as the principal I included reminders in morning announcements. In the weeks when we began to target this behavior, I also broadcast reminder messages a few minutes before the nutrition breaks. Again, staff understood what they were looking for and knew how to redirect student behaviors if necessary. Everyone was being primed to remember that they were responsible for not making a mess and cleaning up their own garbage. It took a few weeks, but eventually I was able to cut back on the reminders and the students were able to meet expectations. Our cleanup time is reduced, so we can use the gym sooner and my custodian was happier and felt his concerns were addressed.

Neither the garbage in the lunchroom nor the ability to walk in the hallways was a bullying behavior, but they became the motivation for the educational professionals in my schools to become involved in redirecting behaviors. As each small misbehavior is tackled, staff becomes more actively involved and more confident in their ability to be successful in their interventions. Students also very quickly realized that we were not waiting for major disruptions to pay attention but instead were watching all the time.

SELF-REFLECTION

Deal with your molehills before they become mountains. Think about the "broken windows" in your school:

1. _____

   _____

2. _____

   _____

3. _____

   _____

4. _____

   _____

The Biggest "Broken Window": The Internet

In our schools and in our homes we now have one of the biggest "broken windows" imaginable. The Internet is literally the entire world at our fingertips. It is a window to fascinating and amazing things, as well as to information and people that our students should never be exposed to. Media literacy and critical literacy skills are of vital importance in schools; at the same time unsafe, inappropriate Internet usage must be one of our "broken windows" for all students, even those in junior kindergarten.

SELF-REFLECTION

What small and tangible steps are needed to address the Internet as a "broken window"?

_____

_____

_____

THE COUNTERARGUMENT: WHAT IF IT'S NOT THE "WINDOWS"?

As with everything there is another side to the story, and the counterarguments to the Broken Windows theory need to be considered too. Levitt and Dubner wrote perhaps the most contentious counterargument to the Broken Windows theory in their book *Freaknomics* (2005). They put forward the thought that the decline in crime in the early 1990s was more a result of legalizing abortion in the 1970s than of targeting petty crimes. They argued that after *Roe v. Wade*, the number of unwanted pregnancies dropped substantially, with a ripple effect that fewer unloved children entered their criminal prime in the 1990s. There is no denying that having fewer children born to what were generally single, uneducated women would have an effect several decades later. What this counterargument doesn't explain is why, despite the decrease in unwanted children, two decades later we have the same amount or even more bullying in our schools. What may be a valid counterargument in the world outside of the education silo does not seem to transfer into the educational framework. That is not to say that the Broken Windows theory is not without its flaws in our educational world too. As educational professionals we would be naïve not to ask, "What if it's not the 'windows'?"

The question "What if it's not the 'windows'?" popped into my head when I began thinking about what to say when you've tried everything and nothing seems to work. As a principal, what do I say to the "but" that seems to follow every "yes" answer I receive? When despite our targeting of our "broken windows," we still have a few students who cannot seem to conform or a few staff members who still cannot intervene, what is the answer? Even in small, rural schools this can be a problem, and I remember thinking that I should just mark an *X* on the wall in my office and bang my head against it when one particular student could not walk quietly down the right-hand side of the hallway. This first-grade student, whom I'll call Justin, could not seem to stop himself from yelling out or hitting other students, even with the teacher right there. Justin was in a class with several students in the autism spectrum, and even the student with the most severe autism was managing, with support, to get through the hallways quietly. Justin, however, was not. In Justin's case, walking quietly did not appear to be the "window."

Justin is just like many of our students. In fact he and his counterparts are the reason that, as educational professionals, we have an extensive alphabet of acronyms. Mental illness and all of its related issues are very much present in our schools. I would have had about as much success with Justin by banging my head against the *X* on my office wall as anything else we would have tried. It turned out, after many appointments with doctors and specialists, that Justin had oppositional defiance disorder (ODD), a very frustrating diagnosis. ODD may seem to justify bad behavior, but it involves much more than behaving badly. ODD is the inability to conform on even the most basic level. Focusing on a "broken window" for a student like Justin is the equivalent of waving a red flag in front of a very angry bull.

It is important to remember that in your school's student body, and quite probably on your staff, you have any number of people who suffer from a range of mental illnesses and other disorders. These can include attention deficit disorder, attention deficit hyperactivity disorder, oppositional defiance disorder, anger management issues, conduct disorders, communication disorders, eating disorders, depression, obsessive-compulsive disorder, bipolar disorder, fetal alcohol syndrome, and, more prevalent lately, fetal methamphetamine syndrome.

There is no panacea for mental illness, and in our youngest students, it is very difficult to diagnose and support. Focusing on "broken windows" will have very little effect on these students' behaviors, and it is essential that students are not punished for behaviors that are beyond their control. I like to illustrate this point with the example I heard early in my teaching career when working with students with learning disabilities, which I'm sure we have all heard: providing support to a student who needs it is like letting a student who needs glasses wear them. We all know that "fair" and "equal" are not the same thing when it comes to providing academic support to students. It is important to remember that mental illness is invisible but real and that these students need our help and support to understand how to function in society.

CASE STUDY: WHAT IS YOUR LINE IN THE SAND?

In Chapter 2 you were asked if you could spot the bully in a group of four students. Evan was identified as a physical bully. Now examine his more extensive biography below to determine what your starting point might be with Evan and his family. Consider using a version of the four quadrants put forward by Steven Covey (1989) to categorize the information you read and guide your actions. You will also be introduced to two other students, Cliff and Spencer, who are struggling in the school setting, and to Pauline, who does not appear to be a problem student at school but who does run a website.

Covey Quadrant

Urgent and Relevant	Not Urgent and Relevant
Urgent and Not Relevant	Not Urgent and Not Relevant

Evan is an only child. His mother dropped out of high school when she found out she was pregnant with Evan at the age of 15. Her boyfriend at the time was 20. He married her, and they moved into his parents' basement. Evan is now 7 years old. His parents are still together and now live in a small apartment.

At school Evan is a C student who is capable of learning, but he has a great deal of difficulty behaving appropriately in class. He has struggled with being able to make good choices since junior kindergarten and, in fact, spent most of his "carpet time" sitting in a hula hoop to help maintain his personal space. He makes physical contact with any student who is near him in the classroom, the hallway, the yard, and the lunchroom. He is brought in off the yard on a daily basis and is often removed from class for making physical contact.

Evan has been on a behavior contract for the past two months and has shown no improvement. Evan also now does not want to come to school because he says no one likes him and they think he is bad. Evan's parents feel their child is being labelled and picked on by all of the teachers. His mother, aunt, and grandmother have all been in the office yelling and screaming at you regarding how Evan is being bullied. His parents' actions are random, sometimes supportive of the schools and sometimes supportive of Evan.

Recently Evan has been expressing behaviors that are sexually more mature than those of his peers. He uses the term hottie *when referring to girls in the class and his teacher. He has also tried to stroke the thigh of a girl in his class and was observed "dry humping" the doorway. When these actions were addressed in a meeting with his parents, they laughed in response and said he saw his uncle doing the same thing to his girlfriend.*

Now try the same exercise with Cliff, a Grade 3 student at your school. He is the middle child, and all three siblings attend your school. Cliff has been diagnosed with ADHD and has been on a variety of medications for the past few years. The medications appear to be ineffective at controlling his impulsivity. Testing indicates that he is of average intelligence, although he is completely illiterate, lacking any number or letter recognition.

Cliff's mother has recently remarried, and his stepfather is now an active and positive part of his life. Cliff's mother is physically disabled due to obesity hampering her ability to walk, and she is also developmentally delayed. Cliff is habitually late, and he and his siblings are reported to the attendance officer on a yearly basis. When Cliff is present, he is unable to work without one-on-one supervision and is a constant fixture at the office following recesses.

Cliff has extensive academic supports in place, but despite being on a modified program, he is unable to succeed academically. Recently he has become more and more disrespectful in the classroom, and his behaviors are escalating at home and in the community.

Consider Spencer. Spencer is in Grade 9 but has become a nonattender. He is gifted and in the 99th percentile in all areas. He has one younger brother who is also extremely gifted but is also rapidly becoming a nonattender. Spencer's father left last year and has remarried. His mother spiraled into a depression at that time and now refuses to leave the house, spending all her time on the Internet. While Spencer does not attend class, he does come to your school everyday and simply hangs out in various locations throughout the building. He is polite to the adults but is sexually degrading in his interactions with female students. He has not been physically abusive but refers to them as "sluts" and "whores."

Pauline is a top Grade 12 student, a good athlete, and a student council member and is popular. In the school building she is a positive role model. She is polite and respectful to all of the staff and well liked by the students. She is a leader within the school community.

Pauline is the youngest in her family, and her three older siblings are all at university. Her parents are both professionals who work long hours to afford a nice house, nice cars, and university tuition.

Pauline started up her own website last year called YouCanBeMyDaddy .com through which she provides both online and in-person services to men. The school became aware of this activity when some of the male students came across the website and posted explicit still photos of Pauline, from her website, around the school.

ACTION: DOTMOCRACY

Main Activity:

Post around the room on pieces of paper the different types of negative behaviors in which students may engage, listed below in no particular order. Some of these behaviors are bullying behaviors, and some are not. There are also behaviors that are applicable to some age groups more than others. You may wish to edit the list by either adding or removing behaviors to suit the age level of the students at your school.

- Behavior that infringes on the rights and/or safety of others
- Running in the halls
- Unprovoked assault on a teacher, student, school employee, or any other person on school property or at school-sponsored events
- Verbal intimidating harassment directed at another person and witnessed
- Extortion or making physical threats to extract favors or money
- Disorderly conduct (throwing snowballs, riding outside a vehicle, etc.) or physical contact (pushing, etc.)
- Possession of toy guns, water balloons, pea shooters, spit wads, and other nonweapon items that when used create minor disruptions
- Using, being under the influence of, or being in possession of alcohol, illegal or nonprescribed drugs, inhalants, look-alike drugs, or paraphernalia on school property or at any school-sponsored activity
- Using or being in possession of tobacco
- Hitting
- Kicking

- Biting
- Slapping
- Pinching
- Shoving
- Pushing
- Tripping
- Spitting
- Punching
- Fighting or provoking a fight
- Inciting others to violence or disobedience
- Loitering in any area for other than intended purposes (bathroom, parking lot, etc.)
- Failure to report directly to the office for disciplinary action
- Being in an unauthorized area without a permit
- Cheating on classroom assignments or test
- Copying or tampering with another person's computer file or a school-owned program/system or any school record
- Indecent exposure (flashing, mooning, etc.)
- Violations of the school dress code
- Disrespect to school official, teacher, or staff employee
- Persistent disobedience
- Rudeness
- Name-calling
- Using racial slurs
- Littering
- Writing graffiti
- Willful destruction or defacement of school property or the property of others
- Skipping class
- Leaving class without permission
- Missing a detention without making alternative arrangements
- Being in the halls without a pass
- Skipping school
- Incurring six or more tardies during one semester
- Setting off false fire alarms
- Making bomb threats
- Engaging in inappropriate displays of affection
- Obscene and/or lewd behavior and/or language (obvious suggestive sexual gestures exhibited in view of students or staff members); profane language (the act of swearing or cursing)
- Lunchroom and bus rule violations

(Continued)

(Continued)

- Misuse of permits or giving false information (the act of illegally using writing, or displaying in writing, the name of another person; falsifying times, grades, addresses, absence excuses, bus notes, or other information on school forms)
- Theft of school property or the property of others
- Possession of prohibited pocket pagers or electronic communication devices

Give each staff member ten stickers. Staff members can place as many stickers on a sheet as they would like. For example, if a teacher feels a behavior is particularly prevalent, he or she may wish to place two or three stickers on that sheet.

The top ten behaviors can be listed on your behavior-reporting sheet in the section "Behavior Problem" to facilitate reporting.

Exit Activity:

Begin to think about what types of consequences would be suitable for the various negative behaviors discussed.

Follow-Up Activity:

Examine your reporting procedures to determine what aspects should remain and what modifications are required. Once the format and content are determined, discuss and determine the implementation process.

- Collate the responses to determine which negative behaviors should be included on the reporting form.
- Create the communication forms/protocols for the school community to use with regard to the new reporting protocol. It is important that the new procedures are clear to both parents and students.

Math Can Make Bystanderism Manageable

THE 80-20 RULE

As an educator, I struggle to understand why things are not getting better in schools despite 30 years of knowing what bullying is. What I have found is that each time I look outside of the silo of education to some other social sciences or behavioral economics idea, my understanding of how to tackle the problems within schools grows. When I started to layer each of my new learnings, my understanding of how to motivate my staff and educate them toward action grew. The bystander effect allowed me understand that bystanderism is not just a school problem, and when I looked at it through the theory of Broken Windows, I began to understand how to make taking action manageable. The 80-20 rule puts in place one more layer of understanding about how to tackle bullying.

At first I didn't know that there was a formal name for the idea that most of the work is done by a few of the people. I had experienced the phenomenon as a teacher when it felt as though only a few of us were running intermural activities or doing extras for the students. I had seen the principle in action as a principal and had even practiced it by continually tapping on the shoulders of the same people whom I knew would say yes. I don't remember how I came across the formal name of the Pareto principle, which is the "law of the vital few": the idea that roughly 80 percent of the effects come from 20 percent of the causes. The principle, which came out of business management, was coined by Joseph M. Juran. Juran named it after the Italian economist Vifredo Pareto, who had observed that 80 percent of the land in Italy was owned by 20 percent of the population. When I flipped the Pareto principle on its head, I began to see how it could be applied in schools. Its application is twofold, with dimensions applicable both to students and to your staff.

In examining students, I realized that if you think of the Pareto principle as it applies to negative behaviors rather than positive ones, you can make a correlation between your student population and bullying. If 80 percent of the effects come from 20 percent of the causes, then it is reasonable that 80 percent of school bullying results from 20 percent of students. Now instead of trying to manage the behaviors of your entire student population, which would be an overwhelming task, you are only managing the behaviors of 20 percent of your students. When the idea of preventing bullying is too big, it causes inaction because our staffs don't know where to start. It becomes unmanageable, and educational professionals thus remain bystanders. Breaking down your school and classrooms into the 80 percent/20 percent categories can make the situation more manageable, allowing educators to move into a position of action.

The point of this book is to help administrators move their staffs toward action, and this is where the second application of the Pareto principle comes into play. Administrators can create the potential for action by making situations more manageable, as previously noted, but they can also use the 80 percent/20 percent idea when looking at their staffs to differentiate their support. We can target those staff members who are in need of more support.

DOING THE MATH

Doing the math is a good place to start. The caution that comes with doing the math is that it doesn't work every time and you can't ignore the students whom you identify as being in the 80 percent group. The Pareto principle is only a theory, and in reality you will find variance from its posited ideal. However, invoking the 80/20 rule will start conversations, which are in and of themselves very valuable, and it will again help move the educational professionals in your buildings from bystander to action by making their role more explicit, tangible, and manageable.

If you look at a school that has 500 students through the lens of the Pareto principle, you get the following:

500 students   80%: 400 students with no major behavior problems

20%: 100 students with behavior problems

Now, instead of trying to monitor every student in your building, your focus is on only 100 students. This is much more manageable than 500 students. Of course, of those 100 students who demonstrate problem behaviors, some will be one-time offenders or will be caught committing minor misbehaviors, while others demonstrate serious problem behaviors repeatedly. If we use the Pareto principle again on the group of 100 students with behavior problems, we get an even more unambiguous understanding of which students require increased attention:

100 students   80%: 80 students with medium-level behavior problems

20%: 20 students with serious behavior problems

As the math shows, with each layering of the 80/20 rule, you can achieve a more targeted approach to the problem of bullying. Instead of 500 students to focus on, you now can focus on 20 students who are exhibiting hard-to-manage or intense misbehaviors.

Now take your challenging 20 students and do the math one more time:

20 students   80%: 16 students with hard-to-manage/intense behavior problems

20%: 4 students with extreme behavior management needs

Doing the math allows you and your staff to narrow your focus from 500 students to 20 students with approximately 4 of these in serious need of support and intervention. Even in a school of 1,000 or 2,000 students, you are targeting 8 to 16 students with intense or extreme behavioral needs. Again, you cannot ignore the rest of the student population, but you can focus on those students with extreme behaviors and bring them to the attention of every staff member.

Using the math to help individual teachers target their attention in their own classrooms can look like this:

Primary class: 80%: 16 students with no behavior problems
20 students
20%: 4 students with behavior problems

4 students	80%: 3 students with moderate behavior problems
	20%: 1 student with intense behavior management needs
Junior class: 30 students	80%: 24 students with no behavior problems
	20%: 6 students with behavior problems
6 students	80%: 4 students with moderate behavior problems
	20%: 2 students with intense behavior management needs
Intermediate/ Secondary rotary: 100 students*	80%: 80 students with no behavior problems
	20%: 20 students with behavior problems

*As students move between classes

20 students	80%: 16 students with moderate behavior problems
	20%: 4 students with intense behavior management needs

This is not to say that sometimes problems will come from other students or that the numbers will always work out exactly, but in general only a handful of students need extra monitoring, supervision, and attention.

SELF-REFLECTION

Think about how the math works in your school. How will you share who the students with behavior problems are with your staff but at the same time avoid labeling these students?

Math: _____

_____

_____

Sharing of information: _____
_____
_____

Avoiding the label: _____
_____
_____

MORE MATH: THE 2-BY-10 STRATEGY

The Pareto principle is a good strategy to make the number of targeted students more manageable for staff. Highlighting those students who need an extra set of eyes on them helps staff move from being bystanders to taking action because they have a better idea of whom to observe. What the numbers up until this point don't tell us is how to make a difference.

It is essential to remember that for each of the numbers you wrote down in the previous section, there is a child in need. Whether that child is 6 or 16, he or she is still a child, and our job is to help that student make the best choices possible. It can be easy in our educational world, which is overrun with data, to forget that each number has a face and a story and deserves to be treated as more than just a statistic.

The 2-by-10 strategy is a way to make a difference using the numbers. The strategy was first introduced by Susan Nolen and her colleagues from the University of Washington (2007) through her research focused on student teachers; Nolen challenged teachers to spend 30 minutes outside of class connecting with students who are at risk. The work of Wlodkowski (1999) further simplified the idea of taking the time to connect with students by saying that the 30 minutes do not have to be consecutive. Just 2 minutes a day for 10 or 15 days can achieve the same result of a deeper understanding of the student and the beginnings of a connection that can change the trajectory of the student's educational future. Thus, we arrive at the 2-by-10 strategy, or 2 minutes a day for 10 days.

I'm not naïve enough to think that 30 minutes is enough to make a difference for every student or that every student is even open to connecting with an adult in school. The 2-by-10 strategy does not mean that you sit down for one heart-to-heart and think that everything will be better. Rather it means that by communicating in small, manageable increments, educational professionals can start to make connections with at-risk students. This strategy also does not mean that you do not connect with all of the students in your class or school. It just means that by giving a student an extra "hello" or having a brief and seemingly superficial encounter in the hallway, you can begin to start something with an at-risk student. Those students may begin to feel a connection with you on a personal level, which may help them see that an adult in their world cares about them. Even in the overworked world of educators, finding two minutes is possible, and that is the true beauty of this philosophy. You don't have to convince your staff to be counselors and have deep and involved sessions with troubled kids. By making such connections manageable, this strategy motivates educators to take action.

As a school administrator, I try to "walk my talk" as much as possible, but there is no denying that it is difficult to do when the papers are piling up and my voice mail light is flashing. Nonetheless, implementing the 2-by-10 strategy can be done in my school. I try to make it a point to let every student have a chance to say hi to me each day. With only 300 students in my building, this goal is doable. I make it a point to go through my lunchrooms and to try to have very brief interactions with as many students as possible. The core of this strategy is the superficiality of it—not that the premise is superficial or that the interactions are superficial to students but that the interactions are quick and not deep in nature. Nonetheless, though your interactions are brief, students must see them as genuine. Smiles and hellos can make a difference as long as the students feel that they are real and that you are happy to see them. In the afternoon, I also make a point of walking at least half of my classrooms. Again, I'm barely in any room for more than three minutes, so I can cover quite a few classrooms and have contact with quite a few students in a relatively short period of time. The second purpose that the walks serve is that students and staff begin to have the impression that I am everywhere. The few minutes that I spend on a daily basis making connections and being visible saves me hours of other problems. This strategy is manageable in larger schools as well if you break them up into sections.

SELF-REFLECTION

What can the 2-by-10 strategy look like for you and your staff in your building?

You: _____

_____

_____

_____

Staff: _____

_____

_____

_____

EVEN MORE MATH: THE MULTIPLIER EFFECT

Math and economics are by no means my areas of expertise. However, the analogy of dropping a small pebble into water and seeing the waves ripple out is well within my grasp. Think about a teacher making a connection with just one student and how that initial effort will have exponential results. The two minutes it takes to create a connection with one student goes well beyond that student. That connection ripples to the student's friends and peer group and family unit. The chain reaction that occurs when a student begins to feel connected, with either a teacher or the school itself, multiplies the impact of the two minutes and the brief connection with each student.

CAN WE CHANGE LIVES?

Can we change lives? I think the answer is a resounding yes, but I know there are times that, as educational professionals, we feel as though we are experiencing chaos theory rather than the multiplier effect. It becomes challenging to target our efforts and measure our results when we are talking about something as vague how connected students feel to staff and how those connections change their life trajectories. As educational professionals, we sometimes get the heartwarming experience of a former student returning and telling us what a difference we made. We hope that we make that difference for every student, but we don't get the qualitative feedback very often.

I know that as a first-year teacher, I had the chance to talk to another teacher who made a huge difference in my schooling. I took my Grade 10 English credit in summer school, and it was one of the most brutal courses I ever took. The teacher was unyielding and taught the course at an insanely rapid pace. It was in this course that I was first introduced to fabulous literature such as *To Kill a Mockingbird* by Harper Lee and pushed to write papers with a depth of analysis beyond anything I had ever done. I would slave over papers only to have them returned covered in harsh red slashes and critiques. At the time I hated this particular teacher. Every time he returned work, I would cringe, but gradually over the course of the summer the red marks lessened, and I began to realize that I could write. I met this particular teacher again when I was a substitute teacher at his high school. I recognized him immediately but said nothing. I was there for two weeks, and it took me the full two weeks to work up the courage to tell him who I was and what an influence he had been on me. Of course he didn't remember me, and for a moment I was crushed. What I took away from that interaction at the time, and again within the framework of this book, made a profound difference in my interactions with my students.

On a personal level, I tried to make connections with my students so that years later I would have a chance to remember them. I say with some pride that while I don't frequently recognize former students when they first come up and say hi, so far I have remembered something about each of the students. They are always much taller and more adult looking than I ever imagined them becoming when they were young, but when I really look in their eyes I can see the kids I knew. Seeing how happy they are when I remember them makes me proud and reminds me that through my interactions, their lives are different.

Writing this book, I began to understand just how influential we are as educational professionals, whether we mean to be or not. My Grade 10 summer school English teacher did not intend to set a direction for my life, but by chance he did. As the responsible adults in the lives of our students, we need to remain very cognizant of the power of our roles. Our actions or lack of actions have an effect. That is a huge responsibility and a huge privilege.

Huge power can bring us a sense of responsibility and privilege, but it can also be so overwhelming that it renders us painfully inactive. The purpose of doing the math is for administrators and educational professionals to realize the power of small changes and small actions. Through incremental changes in our connections with students and our awareness of ourselves, we can move through the five stages of the bystander cycle with more confidence and consistency.

CASE STUDY: WHOM WOULD YOU CHOOSE?

Knowing where to start is often challenging. Here is a sample class of students with brief biographical information on each. Apply the math to figure out whom you need to start to develop a connection with.

Student	Gender	Academic Ability (A, B, C, D)	Race	Behavior Problems (Y/N)	Parental Support (Y/N)	Other
Student A	Male	A	Caucasian	N	Y	Divorced parents
Student B	Male	B+	Caucasian	Y	N	Single mom
Student C	Female	B	Caucasian	N	N	
Student D	Male	A	Asian (Japanese)	Emerging	Y	Recent divorce
Student E	Female	D	Caucasian	N	N	

Student	Gender	Academic Ability (A, B, C, D)	Race	Behavior Problems (Y/N)	Parental Support (Y/N)	Other
Student F	Female	C	Caucasian	N	Y	Hearing impaired
Student G	Female	B	Asian (Pakistani)	N	N	Parents do not speak English.
Student H	Male	B	Half Caucasian/ Half African American	N	Y	
Student I	Male	B–	Caucasian	N	Y	
Student J	Male	D–	Caucasian	Y	N	In foster care
Student K	Male	C	Half Asian (Chinese)/ Half Caucasian	N	N	
Student L	Male	B	Caucasian	Y	Y	Sister with autism
Student M	Female	A	African (Sudanese)	N	N	
Student N	Male	D	Caucasian	Y	Y	Asperger syndrome
Student O	Female	C	Asian (East Indian)	N	N	ESL
Student P	Female	C	Asian (Vietnamese)	N	Y	ESL
Student Q	Male	C	Caucasian	Y	N	
Student R	Female	A	Asian (Vietnamese)	N	N	
Student S	Female	B+	Caucasian	N	N	
Student T	Male	A+	Caucasian	Y	Y	Has been suspended five times this year alone

Remember that you need at least two weeks to develop the beginnings of a bond with a student using the 2-by-10 strategy. For which student would you start to find an extra two minutes? Why that student? Which student would you not pick as a priority? Why would that student not be at the top of your list?

ACTION: MATH, MATH, AND EVEN MORE MATH

Warm-Up Activity:

Work with your entire staff to apply the Pareto principle to your school. Examine what the numbers look like in your building.

Main Activity:

Have each staff member calculate the numbers for his or her students. Once staff members have looked at the numbers in their own classrooms, have them put names and stories to the numbers. It is important to remind your staff that when sharing the names and stories of students, it is essential to be respectful and confidential. The purpose of calculating the numbers and sharing the student stories is not to label or categorize the students negatively but rather to begin to identify students with whom connections are needed.

Once each class has been individually examined, the staff should discuss the highlighted students, first in smaller groups and then as a whole.

Exit Activity:

Ask your staff members to pick one student with whom they will try to make a specific connection over the next few weeks.

Follow-Up Activity:

The Safe Schools Team should collect and collate all the names of students at risk for negative behaviors. This is a large undertaking, but the information they gain will be very useful. This list needs to be revisited frequently, and staff need to provide feedback as to how their efforts to make connections with specific students are going.

Supervision of
Students

MEETING MYLES

I first heard Myles's story when his dad, Mike, came to speak at my school. That's not entirely true. I vaguely remember the story from the news coverage during my first year teaching. In truth, the story was barely a blip on my radar, except I remembered that workers were in the school to redo all the coat hooks in the hallways and bathrooms. I felt awful after I heard Mike speak for the first time; I realized then that something that had been nothing to me had been so incredibly heartbreaking and life changing for him. I felt like dirt and was almost embarrassed to look him in the eye and see the passion that he held so close to his heart. After meeting Mike and hearing him talk about his son, I realized how important it is that this story, and for that matter the story of all victims, is really heard.

Myles was a kid who had never been bullied. He was a happy, well-liked boy whose nickname was in fact "Smiley." He came from a good family and loved school. He lived in Chatham, Ontario, and attended a small school. He had everything going for him, and then one day, February 6, 1998, because of the actions of some of his classmates, he was hanged on the coat hook on the back of a bathroom stall door and never returned home. This tragedy did not happen in a rough inner-city school; Myles attended a small preK–6 school.

Mike still talks about all the moments that are frozen in his mind from that morning. He talks about he felt when he arrived at the school and how his blood ran cold. He tells of how he was treated by the staff and police as he was given the dreadful news. The heartbreak is, as you can imagine, still raw, yet it is tempered with an understanding and a belief that the students responsible for Myles's death did not understand the consequences of their actions and that no true malice was intended.

One of the most powerful parts of Mike's presentation is not when he talks about how the two other boys had permission to be helping a teacher but the teacher wasn't actually there supervising them. It is not when he talks about the fact that other teachers on staff saw the two boys unsupervised and didn't stop to see what they were doing. In fact, he doesn't hold any anger toward the teachers at all. He, if anything, feels a huge amount of compassion for the guilt and grief that they live with. The part of his presentation that sticks in my mind is when he talks about how one of the staff members tried to comfort him with the statement "Myles was just in the wrong place at the wrong time." Mike acknowledges that this statement was probably said with the best of intentions. He knows that it is almost impossible to think of what to say to a grieving parent. But think about that statement: "He was in the wrong place at the wrong time." Think about it. That statement couldn't have been more wrong, in Canada or anyplace else. In fact, "everyday, over 52 million children attend 114,000 schools in the United States, and when combined with the 6 million adults working in schools, almost one-fifth of the population in the U.S. are to be found in schools on any given week" (Huang et al., 2005, p. 623). That statement was so painfully wrong. Myles was exactly where he was supposed to be. He was where his parents were legally mandated to send him until the age of 16. Myles had permission from the duty teacher to be in the washroom. He had followed all the rules and was just going about his day.

What Myles's story reminds us as educators is that parents send us their kids. Our lives get so busy in the office that we frequently can fall into the trap of seeing kids only as numbers. I know that in the previous chapter, we used math to make the insurmountable problem of bullying more manageable, but the numbers must always be tempered by the face of humanity. The numbers that meet the cap size, the number of Individualized Education Plans, the standardized test scores, and more numbers—we live in a world of numbers. Not to be dismissive of our roles as educators because, yes, it's great if children learn stuff while they are in our buildings. Yes, we have to be the instructional leaders in our buildings and support student learning. More than that, however, we have a duty to return each and every kid that a parent sends to us safely at the end of every day. Hopefully, we improve them, teach them, and nurture them. But at the very minimum we have a duty to keep them physically and emotionally safe.

I used to get offended in my early days of teaching when people would tell me that I "couldn't understand" because I didn't have kids. Older teachers would give me a "there-there" pat on the head type of look and tell me that I'd be a better teacher once I had kids. I would get beyond furious with them and insist indignantly that I was a good teacher. And I was a good teacher. Reluctantly, I now admit that they were probably right. In my case, I am a better administrator because I have kids. Despite being sleep deprived most of the time, I have more patience and empathy than before Zoe and Ewan arrived. Now, without meaning to or even really being conscious of it, I see Zoe's face in that of every little girl and Ewan's face in that of every little boy who arrives at my office. I try to treat students the way I want my children to be treated when they arrive at the office. The most frustrating thing I hear is an educator responding to a student by saying, "Did you tell the duty teacher?" or "Did you tell your classroom teacher?" Yes, taking time for everything that lands on your plate is tough, but when the consequences are as serious as potentially losing the life of a student, those two minutes are beyond valuable.

SELF-REFLECTION

Empathy is powerful. How can you inspire it in the educational professionals in your school? How do every bully and every bullied student have a face and voice?

_____

_____

_____

_____

_____

IT'S NEVER THE "WRONG PLACE"

A student who is bullied is not in the wrong place because there is no right place for bullying. However, bullying is a reality in our schools, and the results of my research indicate that educational professionals are at all stages in their abilities to intervene in bullying episodes. The predominant problem remains a lack of awareness, not a lack of caring or willingness to intervene. This lack of awareness is causing the adults in schools to be unconsciously incompetent with regard to their roles in bullying situations. The results are negative for both the educational professional and the students.

The students suffer regardless of the role they play in bullying episodes. The bullied, 12 to 15 percent of students (Pepler, Craig, Ziegler, & Charach, 1994), are typically very unhappy children who suffer from fear, anxiety, and low self-esteem as a result of the bullying. They may try to avoid school, and even avoid all social interaction, in an effort to escape the bullying. Some victims of bullying are so distressed that they commit, or attempt to commit, suicide.

There are also consequences for the bully. Bullies tend to become aggressive adults who stand a much higher chance than average of incurring multiple criminal convictions (Olweus, 1978). These findings by Olweus and his group fit well with those of other studies, which have found exactly the same outcome for children, especially males, who are aggressive as children (Loeber & Dishion, 1983; Robins, 1978).

Finally, the student bystanders also suffer from negative consequences. The bullying may cause anxiety or fear in bystanders. The learning environment is poisoned by bullying, particularly when no effective interventions take place. Children who observe violent behavior and see that it has no negative consequences for the bully will be more likely to use aggression themselves in the future (Sudermann, Jaffe, & Schieck, 1996).

Just as student bystanders can experience anxiety and fear, so too can adult bystanders. The personal consequences of bullying include absence from work and emotional and stress-related symptoms, including increased fear, loss of sleep, loss of self-confidence, anxiety, loss of appetite, and depression (Elementary Teachers' Federation of Ontario & Ontario English Catholic Teachers' Association, 2006).

With negative outcomes for everyone involved in bullying episodes, the implications are of paramount importance. Schools need to make schools the right place for everyone to work and learn in physical and emotional safety. What is currently occurring in schools is not good enough, and the training that educational professionals are currently receiving is not sufficient. Adults in the school buildings cannot remain as bystanders, and a lack of awareness cannot be an acceptable excuse. As Twemlow (2001) argued, the role of the bystander should not be underestimated. The bystander can be regarded as the "invisible engine in the cycle of bullying." Twemlow highlighted the contribution of adults to creating an environment where bullying can either diminish or flourish in school communities; he emphasized the importance of adults modeling positive behaviors in all their interactions with pupils and each other to set an example. Research has clearly demonstrated that bystanders play a significant role in bullying.

Thus, proactive and preventative interventions implemented at the individual, class, school, and community level have the potential to reduce bullying. These are critical alongside reactive strategies to deal with bullying incidents when they occur. We adults must also recognize our own bystanding behaviors and seek to model positive actions by looking at our own "systems, structures and policies and do some audits and research into how they may be framing, perpetuating and justifying bullying and harassment amongst students" (Martino & Pallotta-Chiarolli as quoted in "Bullying. No Way!" 2009; see also Martino & Pallotta-Chiarolli, 2005). The data from my 2008 survey indicate that as educational professionals reflect upon their own bystanding behaviors, they will find that both structural and attitudinal barriers exist.

The adults in school buildings need to be able to decide to intervene quickly in order to move from the bystander role. Targeted support ensures that all educational professionals can develop an understanding of their roles and how essential they are to stopping bullying. However, just as the decision-making process has multiple steps, so too does the process to initiate and sustain change.

UNDERSTANDING THE RESPONSIBILITY OF SUPERVISION

For a school administrator, the weight of the responsibility of supervision can be overwhelming. The challenge is helping educational professionals move through the Continuum to Action.

The third step in the decision to help in a bullying situation is that the bystander must determine the extent to which he or she has the responsibility to help (Huston, Ruggiero, Conner, & Geis, 1981). As discussed in Chapter 3, the respondents to my 2008 survey were asked to indicate which of a list of reasons they would give for not intervening in a bullying situation. (see Tables 3.1 and 3.2). They were also given the same statements but asked to project why they felt others would not intervene. Positive responses to statements such as "I didn't want to get involved," "I wasn't the person on duty," and "I told the students to talk to the teacher on duty" indicate that a portion of the respondents did not feel they had a responsibility to help. The percentage of positive responses was substantially higher for these three statements when the respondents were asked to hypothesize about others than when they self-assessed. Only slightly more than 1 percent of respondents indicated "I didn't want to get involved" was a reason they themselves would not intervene, yet over 50 percent indicated that the statement was true for their colleagues. Just over 5 percent of respondents indicated "I wasn't the person on duty" as a reason for nonintervention, but over 50 percent indicated that the statement was true for their colleagues. Finally, 22.2 percent passed the responsibility of intervention to someone else, indicating that "I told the students to talk to the teacher on duty." However, the respondents hypothesized that their colleagues pass on the responsibility to intervene 52.4 percent of the time.

In this set of data responses, as in all previous steps, it becomes evident that all categories include a portion of the respondents. Therefore, some educational professionals are not able to move beyond step 3 and will not intervene in bullying episodes, instead remaining bystanders.

In the decision-making section of the continuum, educational professionals must decide if they have the ability and knowledge to help. This idea was addressed in several areas of my research. I asked respondents to respond to the statement "I didn't know what to do or who to talk to," with regard to why they would not intervene in bullying episodes and why they believed colleagues might not intervene. Slightly more than 5 percent of respondents indicated that they themselves did not know what to do or whom to talk to, and they hypothesized that 31.8 percent of their colleagues did not know what to do or whom to talk to when they witnessed a bullying incident. Respondents were also asked if they felt comfortable implementing an antibullying or antiharassment program. In self-assessment, 25.7 percent indicated "no" or "unsure," and when assessing colleagues, again over a quarter of respondents, 32.2 percent, indicated "no" or "unsure."

The answers to these questions indicate that at least a quarter of the educational professionals in the schools do not feel they know how to help. As a result, they are not able to move from the role of bystander when witnessing bullying episodes.

In addition to having the correct training and knowing the appropriate protocol to provide help, the bystander must feel he or she has the power to intervene (Huston et al., 1981). Some educational professionals may have the necessary training but lack the confidence to act; they may find themselves not only in the role of bystander but in that of victim. Many of the respondents in my research indicated that they were victims of both verbal (52.4%) and physical (4.2%) bullying themselves by colleagues. They also indicated that they experienced verbal (56.6%) and physical (14.3%) bullying from students, as well as verbal (72.0%) and physical (3.6%) bullying from parents. The combination of feeling unsafe and being bullied themselves will prevent many educational professionals from intervening in bullying episodes, as they themselves will suffer from many of the side effects of being bullied and therefore will lack the belief that they possess the power to help. Moreover, many respondents (12.1%) indicated that they felt they would not be supported if they intervened in a bullying episode. The idea of support was further addressed in question 16, which asked respondents to evaluate the level of support they received from parents and colleagues. Of respondents, 56.5 percent felt that they were never, rarely, or only sometimes supported in the intervention and actions by parents. Almost 27 percent felt they were rarely or sometimes supported by their colleagues. Educational professionals were also asked if they felt safe at school; in self-assessment, 11.1 percent responded either "no" or "unsure," and when asked to predict if their colleagues felt safe at school, 18.1 percent either were unsure or did not think their colleagues felt safe.

Stage 4 in the decision-making process is perhaps the most challenging for educational professionals. They are able to identify that something abnormal is happening, that help is needed, and that they have a responsibility to help. However, due to a lack of confidence and because they feel unsafe, unsupported, and victimized, they do not feel they have the skills to intervene successfully.

Over the past few years in Ontario, the number of negotiated supervision minutes has steadily decreased, creating supervision gaps; these are detrimental to the well-being of students (Ontario Principals' Council, 2007). As the Elementary Teachers' Federation of Ontario continues to negotiate for lower supervision minutes for its members, clearer supervision standards must be established. Supervision of children has been found to be of prime importance. Just as low levels of supervision in the home are associated with the development of bullying problems in individual children (Loeber & Stouthamer-Loeber, 1986; Olweus, 1993; Patterson, DeBaryshe, & Ramsey, 1989), so too are low levels of supervision at school, particularly on the playground or in the schoolyard and in the hallways. Also, the appropriateness of interventions by adults when they see bullying or are made aware of it is very important (Sudermann et al., 1996).

The Ontario Principals' Council has recommended 12 standards to be implemented in all schools, with the first being that only trained staff shall be given supervisory duties. The key word in that statement is *trained*. School administrators have explicit expectations with regard to how literacy, mathematics, and other subject areas are to be taught and assessed. The expectations are clearly communicated to staff via inservices, and the implementation of best practices is supervised and evaluated. However, it has been my observation that the same practice does not occur with regard to supervisory duties. A schedule is created, honoring the minutes of the collective agreements, but no instruction is provided as to how the supervision is to occur. Based on the data, I suggest that one cannot assume that educational professionals are aware of what active supervision entails. For example, many are clearly unaware of the bullying that occurs in their schools. I propose that it is the responsibility of the school administrator to educate staff that being on duty is more than being physically present for the required number of minutes; it is actively moving around the entire supervision area and actively observing interactions between students.

SELF-REFLECTION

What is your understanding of supervision? Have you shared your thoughts with your staff? Have you considered or implemented best practices for supervision?

_____

_____

_____

_____

As you begin to think about supervision, you may realize that you now have more questions than answers. Your questions may be as broad as "What is supervision?" to the specific details of "Must a student be within your range of sight? Within hearing? In physical proximity?" You may be wondering, "Is it ever okay to have students working in a classroom when an adult is not in the room with them, or can an educator send a student into the hallway?" This questioning and the process of coming to a consensus about supervision beliefs are just as important as arriving at answers because the answers are only right when everyone agrees with them and implements them with consistency. The answers below are only, and I repeat _only_, starting points.

What is supervision? According to the Family and Children's Aid Services of Waterloo Region (n.d.) in Ontario, _supervised_ is defined as when "the caregiver can see the child and is close enough to protect the child from harm" (¶ 1). The Texas Department of Family and Protective Services (n.d.) defines _neglectful supervision_ as "placing a child in or failing to remove a child from a situation that a reasonable person would realize requires judgment or actions beyond the child's level of maturity, physical condition or mental abilities and that results in bodily injury or substantial risk of immediate harm to the child" ("What is neglectful supervision?") As educational professionals, we act as the parent when the students are in our care. Therefore, both definitions can be translated as follows: _supervision is when the educational professional can see the student and is close enough to protect the student from harm_. This definition is sufficiently broad to cover all situations and age groups, but its very generality is why the answer is only the starting point for the conversation among staff members.

Bullying 24/7

It used to be that once students left school and made it home, they were safe from bullying. Advances in technology have changed that. Bullying has become a 24/7 epidemic. Students can e-mail, upload, tweet, and text 24 hours a day, 7 days a week from anywhere. Closing the door no longer keeps the bullies out or stops their ability to hurt.

In this new virtual world that our students live in, it becomes very challenging to address bullying because it can happen anytime and anywhere. The Internet also provides the bully the option of anonymity and makes it very difficult to see where the role of bystander exists. Supervision in a borderless world is a new challenge for educational professionals. Our role in bullying that exists beyond our school walls is a gray area. However, in Ontario under the new Safe Schools legislation, if an educational professional becomes aware of an activity that has a negative impact on the school climate, he or she has a duty to report the information to the principal.

CASE STUDY: SPOT THE SUPERVISION PROBLEM

Read each of the scenarios below and try to spot the supervision problem. Consider also if you would class the problem as small, medium, or large. Then read the "twist" and see how that affects your classification. Once you have determined what the problem is, think about what would constitute proper supervision in each situation.

Scenario 1: The teacher leaves a class unattended to go to the washroom in the middle of period 2.

Small   Medium   Large

Twist: The class is in a temporary building outside of the main school building.

Scenario 2: High school students are on a year-end trip to a nearby major city. They have "free time" and are told to meet with their chaperone at 3:00 P.M.

Small   Medium   Large

Twist: During their "free time," the students go to a strip club and are served alcohol.

Scenario 3: The teacher on duty arrives at his or her duty post five minutes late.

Small   Medium   Large

Twist: While the yard is unsupervised, a fight breaks out, and a student requires medical attention.

Scenario 4: While in the computer lab, the teacher does not have direct sightlines on all of the computer screens.

Small   Medium   Large

Twist: Students access pornographic materials via the Internet.

Scenario 5: During class time, the teacher is checking e-mail and not watching or engaging with students as they work.

Small   Medium   Large

Twist: Two students sneak out of class, leave school property, and are arrested for shoplifting.

Scenario 6: The custodian comes across two students smoking pot in one of the back stairwells. He does not interact with the students, and he does not report their behavior.

Small   Medium   Large

Twist: The students drive home under the influence and crash their car. No one is hurt, but they admit to everything to avoid criminal charges and state that the custodian witnessed their behavior.

ACTION: SUPER SUPERVISION

Each school will have different supervision needs based on its demographics. It is important to incorporate the information you compiled regarding "hot spots" and "staff-free" zones for your school into your supervision training.

Warm-Up Activity:

Have staff complete a brainstorming session focusing on what they think are the important aspects of student supervision. Use the following questions to help guide the discussion:

- What is one thing you do when on duty that you consider effective, and why do you feel it is effective?
- What would you change about current supervision practices?
- How do you use proactive observation skills when on duty?

Main Activity:

Review your expectations for supervision. These can be developed by yourself and your co-administrators, your supervision committee, your Safe Schools Team, or your entire staff. It is suggested that you include the following ideas.

- **Movement.** When a staff member is on duty, it is important that he or she continually move around the duty area. Staff need to cover the perimeter of their areas, paying special attention to corners or blind spots.
- **Location.** Duty staff need to have a clear understanding of exactly the areas within the school or in the school yard that they are supervising. The areas should be clearly marked on the school map and labeled to match the duty schedule (e.g., Mr. Smith, A.M. duty, section A). Reviewing the areas orally may not be sufficient. Having your staff walk the areas they are responsible for is important so that they have an explicit understanding of their supervision areas. It will also give them an opportunity to look for any blind spots that may be present. *Suggestion:* Have staff complete a scavenger hunt of the different duty areas.
- **Visibility.** Staff members on duty need to be clearly and readily visible to students. You will want to decide as a staff what you can wear to identify yourselves as staff members on duty. For example, orange crossing-guard vests are often used, but you may consider any items that are brightly colored and easy to put on and take off. The item also needs to be able to be visible even when the person is wearing winter clothing for outside duties in cold climates. Once the identifier is chosen, it is important to communicate with all staff members the expectation that they wear the item at all times when on duty.
- **Specific roles.** It is important to specify the roles of on-duty staff (e.g., Staff A is responsible for the doorway when the bell rings, and Staff B sweeps the remainder of the yard to round up straggling students).
- **Rules.** School rules for behavior will vary from school to school, as well as for different locations in the school. As a staff it is important to determine the expectations for behavior in the schoolyard, in the hallways, and in the lunchroom or cafeteria. Once the rules have been determined, it is essential that all staff members are aware of the rules and expectations.
- **Reporting.** Once the rules and expectations have been established, staff need to be aware of how to report any problems to the office in a consistent manner. For reporting to be successful, it must be easy and consistent.

(Continued)

(Continued)

- **Inclusion.** It is important that all staff are included in developing the reporting process and expectations. Office professionals, custodians, and educational assistants all need to be as aware as teachers of behavioral expectations and consequences for negative behaviors. Reporting behaviors to the office is the responsibility of all staff members, regardless of their role within the school. Be sure that your entire staff has behavior-reporting sheets and are aware of how the forms are to be used.
- **More suggestions.** The duty staff can all carry clipboards with reminders regarding movement, visibility, roles, rules, and reporting sheets. This will facilitate understanding and ease of reporting.

  The reporting sheet should always be photocopied on the same color of paper, and that color should not be used for any other purpose.

  File the behavior reports for each student as they are received. This will allow you to determine if the behaviors are isolated and are simply inappropriate or if they constitute consistent, targeted bullying.

The Importance of Being Able to Say What You Mean

WHAT IS MITIGATION?

Mitigated speech is a fancy linguistic term for sugarcoating what you are saying. We all do it. In fact, I would guess that we all do it every day. Fischer and Orasanu (1999) described the degrees of mitigation that exist between two individuals. They came up with six categories ranging from sugar-free to sugar-covered jelly donut.

1. **Command.** "Strategy X is going to be implemented."

2. **Team Obligation Statement.** "We need to try strategy X."

3. **Team Suggestion.** "Why don't we try strategy X?"

4. **Query**. "Do you think strategy X would help us in this situation?"

5. **Preference**. "Perhaps we should take a look at one of these Y alternatives."

6. **Hint.** "I wonder if we could run into any roadblocks on our current course."

OPAQUENESS: THE REAL COST OF LIES IS THAT THEY OBSCURE THE TRUTH

When language is mitigated, the meaning behind the words becomes opaque. The hidden impact of our words is a cost to the safety of the students in our care. That is not to say that we are lying; however, when we are unable to be understood by others, the truth is obscured.

For us, as administrators, when our truths are obscured, the result is the same as if we were to lie. Lying undermines trust in a society, and opaqueness in language can undermine trust among staff members. For example, if I have a conversation with a staff member about my expectations, as the supervisor, regarding wearing the orange yard-duty vest and I mitigate to the point that the person does not realize that I am communicating an expectation, complications can arise that result in a deterioration of our professional relationship. If I say, "I noticed that you were not wearing your yard-duty vest when you were outside on Tuesday," instead of, "Please remember that you are expected to wear your yard-duty vest when you are on an outside duty," the teacher may not realize that I really do expect him or her to wear the vest. This mitigation may seem innocent, but it sets off a ripple effect that becomes a problem. That teacher may not wear the vest during the next yard-duty shift, and I will, no doubt, become very frustrated with that staff member's lack of respect for our common expectations. I no longer trust that he or she will do as I ask. Likewise, the staff member will no longer trust what I say because I was not clear enough and he or she now feels uncertainty around any future conversations.

This subtle deterioration in communication and trust is exponentially increased with each subsequent mitigated conversation. It will also have a negative impact on the staff as a whole because as the lack of trust grows, it will begin to affect all relationships. We have all either worked with or for someone whom we did not trust. Sometimes the reasons for the distrust were very obvious, but often the distrust builds slowly over time through a series of interactions that seem unimportant by themselves. That is the true cost of mitigation.

LESSONS FROM KOREAN AIR

I first read about mitigated speech and the story of Korean Air in *Outliers* by Malcolm Gladwell (2008). He wrote about how mitigated speech is so powerful that it was determined to be the cause of the demise and rebirth of Korean Air in the 1990s. Korean Air had so many plane crashes that it actually lost its status as an airline. Investigation into crash after crash kept coming to the same conclusion. The planes crashed, in general, not because of one catastrophic mistake but the accumulation of lots of smaller mistakes. None of the smaller mistakes were in themselves a problem, but the layering of small mistake upon small mistake was fatal. As researchers started to look at all the small mistakes, they discovered that mitigated speech played an important role. They determined that the

Korean culture of respect for authority was a detriment. Subordinate flight crew members would never try to instruct, correct, or challenge a flight crew member higher up the ladder of authority. Once mitigated speech was corrected, Korean Air rebounded and became the respected airline it is today.

I began reflecting on my reading and wondering, "How does Korean culture and the lesson of mitigated speech link to school culture?" I would love it if we were both cultures rooted in respect for authority. I think we all know that respect does not always prevail in our buildings all the time, but as administrators we always try to deal with people respectfully. At times, that can cause us to mitigate our thoughts extensively. I know that I am guilty of this myself. My out-loud voice and my inside voice often do not say the same thing. This results in a great deal of frustration. My "hints" are not usually successful in changing the problem, and by the second or third conversation with the person, I'm angry and frustrated—and, in fairness, the other person is confused. The other person heard a hint or suggestion, while in my mind I was blunt and commanding. Like many of us, I don't really like having difficult conversations. I'm much more comfortable mitigating my words and sugarcoating things. Will I ever be comfortable having blunt conversations? Probably not. Does my awareness of this part of my personality allow me to make a more conscious effort to be clear? Yes. It is critical that speech is not mitigated when student safety and staff supervision issues are addressed.

The research also found that the more people actively involved in flying the plan, the fewer accidents occurred (Gladwell, 2008). If everyone from the captain to the first officer to the flight engineer to the flight attendants feels active ownership in the success of the flight, then fewer mistakes are made. Little problems can be solved when they are still little problems, before they have a chance to compound into a fatal crash. A community effort gives airlines—and passengers—accident-free flights.

What can the story of the rise and fall of Korea Air teach us about bullying in our schools?

- No more mitigated speech. When it comes to the health and safety of our students, direct communication matters. Enable people to mean what they say and say what they mean without fear of repercussions.
- Deal with problems when they are small. Don't let inconsequential issues compound into critical problems.
- Empower others. Decentralize power and decision making. Involve everyone! Everyone can, if they wish, participate in the health and welfare of the community.

SELF-REFLECTION

Do you mitigate your speech?

_____

_____

_____

Do U Speak Txt?

As adults, we mitigate our speech to be polite. In the world of texting or tweeting, however, mitigation does not exist. Expressing thoughts in 140 characters or less does not leave enough space to sugarcoat what you are saying. Students have an entire language that has evolved, and continues to evolve, at a rapid pace. This abbreviated and coded language is now one of the new languages of bullying. Becoming fluent in "leet-speak" is like learning a foreign language for adults, but being able to understand this language is essential to stop cyber bullying, text bullying, and sext bullying.

You don't need to text or tweet yourself, but as an educational professional, you need to develop a working knowledge of the world in which your students live. When we think about the statistics shared throughout this book regarding lack of awareness, we see that knowledge is important. That knowledge cannot be limited to what occurs in the physical building of the school. It must extend into all the arenas in which bullying exists. A quick Google search of Internet acronyms will give you some of the most used text speak. You can also turn to Resource D for a list that I compiled to get you started.

Following are several examples of cyber bullying:

- Kristy posts a note anonymously on several popular social websites: "Carolyn is a skanky b**tch and a whore."
- Kimmy blue-jacks Ally's phone and sends the following text message to all the boys in the school: IWSN & I want u 2 FMLTWIA.
- Anna uses a photo editor to paste Kevin's face onto a naked body and posts the image to several social websites with the tag line "Tiny banana."

CRUCIAL CONVERSATIONS: THE DANGER OF STORIES

While looking at students simply as numbers has its pitfalls, as I discussed in Chapter 5, so too do the stories we share about students. It becomes very easy for the story to become the truth because it is told so many times. Believing the stories gives them a great deal of power, and they can become mitigating factors for our actions. When we are talking about bullying, each conversation is crucial, and differentiating between fact and fiction is important.

I looked at the topic of priming in Chapter 2, where I shared my stories of Colleen and Chris. I am conscious of some of the ways in which I've been primed, but I also know that I have been primed in other ways of which I am not fully conscious. That unconscious priming causes me, and everyone else, to react to situations on an instinctual level. We are not robots. All of us come with our own histories that influence who we are. People have told me that I am overly politically correct. For example, if someone comments negatively on immigrants, I will quickly and proudly say that I am a first-generation Canadian and that both my parents are immigrants to this country.

We all have our politically correct faces that we wear to the world—I doubt that any of us would stand up and openly admit to being a bigot, a sexist, or a homophobe. We might very well not be any of those things, but human beings are not neutral beings. Priming is incredibly subtle and incredibly powerful. It is so powerful in fact that Professor Claude Steele of Stanford found that when black students were asked to indicate their race on a standardized IQ test before taking the test, their scores dropped (Steele & Aronson, 1995). Simply and very innocuously mentioning race invoked its negative connotations and affected performance. When you think of bullying, what subtle triggers influence your behavior, without your awareness? When you think of certain students in your schools, what influences your thinking? You may have heard comments like "Oh, he's from that family," or "What can you expect from a kid in that neighborhood?" Do you let your preconceived notions influence how attentive you are? Do you hear the stories or the facts?

SELF-REFLECTION

How are you primed: Is it better to come from a poor family in a good neighborhood or school than to be from a good family in a poor neighborhood or school?

_____

_____

_____

CASE STUDY: WHAT WOULD YOU SAY?

In this case study you will revisit the scenarios from Chapter 6 and start to think about what you would say and do in each of the situations. This process of reflection is very complicated, and there are many different answers and solutions. You also need to be aware of the legal ramifications of your action or inaction; you should familiarize yourself with the laws in your area, as well as the stance of your union or professional body.

You can consider the scenarios from two different stances. From the first perspective, you are the adult in each of the scenarios. Think about what you would do to avoid a supervision error. The second, and more challenging, perspective is to think about your actions if you came upon the situation. Consider how you would react in the moment and what types of conversations would need to occur in both the immediate situation and over the next few days or weeks.

Scenario 1: The teacher leaves a class unattended to go to the washroom in the middle of period 2. Twist: The class is in a temporary building outside of the main school building.

Scenario 2: High school students are on a year-end trip to a nearby major city. They have "free time" and are told to meet with their chaperone at 3:00 P.M. Twist: During their "free time," the students go to a strip club and are served alcohol.

Scenario 3: The teacher on duty arrives at his or her duty post five minutes late. Twist: While the yard is unsupervised, a fight breaks out, and a student requires medical attention.

Scenario 4: While in the computer lab, the teacher does not have direct sightlines on all of the computer screens. Twist: Students access pornographic materials via the Internet.

Scenario 5: During class time, the teacher is checking e-mail and not watching or engaging with students as they work. Twist: Two students sneak out of class, leave school property, and are arrested for shoplifting.

Scenario 6: The custodian comes across two students smoking pot in one of the back stairwells. He does not interact with the students, and he does not report their behavior. Twist: The students drive home under the influence and crash their car. No one is hurt but they admit to everything to avoid criminal charges and state that the custodian witnessed their behavior.

ACTION: A COMMON LANGUAGE

You may feel that your staff do not need an activity on common vocabulary—that you already share a common language when talking about bullying. If that is the case, then you may want to use only the scenarios and not the warm-up activity suggestions. However, if you have new staff members, the warm-up activities may be a good starting point for them, as well as useful review for the remainder of your staff.

Warm-Up Activity:

Have your staff complete a "Think, Pair, Share" activity using the keywords *bully*, *bullied*, *bystander*, and *intervener*. Encourage them to write down everything they can think of with regard to the keywords and then share their thoughts with two other staff members before sharing as an entire group. Once everyone has had a chance to reflect on the keywords, you may wish to use the following questions, as appropriate, based on their answers.

1. How many different types of bullying do you think there are?

2. Are there different types of bullied people?

3. What role do you fit into as an educational professional?

Main Activity:

Examine the following scenarios and identify what type of bully, bullied, bystander, or intervener is present. Who are the stakeholders, and what are their short-term and long-term responsibilities?

Scenario 1: You see a student from your class, Valerie, walking down the hallway. She is alone, as usual. She is wearing baggy jeans and a big sweatshirt. Her hair is hanging down around her face, and she is looking down as she walks along the hallway. You watch as she passes another group of students who start flicking pennies at her and calling her names. You can't quite hear everything, but you can make out some of the words. You hear her called a "dyke" and a "lesbo." You notice that she doesn't react. She keeps walking and does not look up or acknowledge the comments in any way.

Scenario 2: You assign group work in your class. As the students move to sit in their groups, you notice that Pardeep moves very slowly to the group to which you assigned him. As he sits down, you see two other students in the group pull their chairs away ever so slightly and cover their noses with their hands. The rest of the group giggles, and those students cover their noses too.

(Continued)

(Continued)

Scenario 3: You are in the lunchroom when you notice that Sarah is purposely moving closer and closer to the other students assigned to her table. She is nudging them with her shoulder and elbow, and her lunch is spreading out into their space. The other students continually move over and push her lunch back toward her. Finally, after this behavior continues for several minutes, Mark loses his temper and dumps her pudding cup onto her lap. Sarah quickly gets up to tell you, as the duty teacher, that Mark is bullying her again.

Scenario 4: You discover that there is a Facebook group called "I Hate Mr. Smith." Students at your school have been joining this group and posting various types of negative comments regarding this teacher. Recently, pictures have been taken with cell phone cameras and posted of Mr. Smith's rear end while he was writing on the board. Other pictures are beginning to appear in which Mr. Smith's face has been digitally copied and pasted onto other images.

Exit Activity:

Suggestion 1: Have your staff complete a survey regarding what types of bullying they think occur in your school.

Suggestion 2: Have your staff complete a survey regarding what they have learned during this activity and on what topics they would like more information.

Follow-Up Activites:

Examine the exit activity completed by your staff to determine what direction your inservices for the year should take.

If your staff completed the survey regarding types of bullying present in your school, examine the data to determine if the results are what you would expect. Use the following questions to begin to guide your discussion.

- Is one type of bullying more prevalent than others?
- Is the distribution of bullying types a result of your school's demographics?
- How can you target your interventions to the types of bullying that are most prevalent in your school?
- Does a particular type of bullying appear to be more prevalent simply because it is more observable?
- Does your staff need support to be able to identify different types of bullying?

If your staff completed the activity to determine what they want to learn more about, you can examine the responses to see if there are trends and areas of interest upon which to base your inservices.

Action at All Levels

SATISFICE IS NOT ENOUGH

Satisfactory will no longer suffice. Satisfice is a dangerous mind-set because it allows us to keep doing what we're doing without understanding the need to try something different. Recall this from the introduction: if we do what we've always done, we'll get what we've always gotten. Clearly, we need to think innovatively at both the school level and beyond. At a systematic level, educators need to think and act differently to remove the structural and attitudinal barriers from all levels of our education system.

The data collected via my research indicate that many educational professionals are unaware of the prevalence and location of bullying in their schools. This lack of awareness creates an opportunity for bullying to continue and must be addressed proactively.

Improve in-faculty teacher training.

The results from this survey support data collected worldwide that have determined educators receive insufficient training in the area of antibullying and that the majority of teachers express a desire for more training (Hanish & Guerra, 2000; Newman, Murray, & Lussier, 2001). In my research, the t test results ($t = .836$) indicate a need for not only more training but a different type of training, since current practice has improved the ability of educational professionals to move out of the role of bystander. Nicolaides, Toda, and Smith (2002) have shown a variation in British trainee teachers' knowledge of bullying that is mirrored in Canada. Teacher training is critical in identifying and responding to bullying (Boulton, 1997; Craig et al., 2000; Townsend-Wiggins, 2001). Yet dealing with school bullying is yet to be implemented as a core unit within preservice education courses.

I suggest that explicit training with regard to active observation skills needs to begin during teacher training and mentored during the first years of teaching to solidify best practices. In-faculty, or inservice, training focuses on how to plan lessons and deliver curriculum. Practicum teaching blocks allow for practice with these skills, and most evaluations also focus exclusively on the ability to deliver curriculum. Yet when students are the victims of bullying, they often suffer from sliding or failing grades, and the work of curriculum development and delivery is undone (Hulley & Dier, 2005). It is essential that the students in the classroom feel safe and respected in order to maximize their academic potential.

Thus, I propose that education curricula include a required course that focuses on bullying to ensure that new teacher graduates have a solid understanding of what it is, what the ramifications are, and their responsibility to both the victim and the bully. Role-playing and case studies would allow prospective educators to understand the wide range of scenarios that constitute bullying behaviors. In addition to learning about the classroom, student teachers need to be taught explicitly how to walk the hallways and playground while actively observing the student interactions around them. To build on this direct instruction during the practicum teaching blocks, I suggest that student teachers practice the skills of actively observing in the hallways and the schoolyard as diligently as they plan the lessons they are to deliver. As noted in Chapter 6, clear supervision standards must be developed, and these should be included in teacher training regarding bullying prevention. Evaluation practices need to encompass not only practical teaching and education theory but also observation and intervention skills the teacher demonstrates wherever bullying might take place.

Include antibullying in the teacher induction program and the teacher performance appraisal process.

In my research, the t tests ($t = .67$) indicate that there is no difference in response to bullying episodes between experienced and inexperienced educational professionals. To create change through pressure, frequent monitoring and assessment is required (DuFour, 2000). Benseman and Comings (2008) demonstrated in their case study that pressure through frequent and formal assessment improves foundational skills in adults.

The same concept can be translated to improving intervention in bullying episodes. Formalizing the assessment process of the educational professional's role in preventing bullying highlights the importance of this issue. Antibullying's specific inclusion in the performance appraisal process also ensures that the educational professional's role be reviewed on a regular and frequent basis. The inclusion of antibullying in the teacher induction program is also essential, as it will draw explicit attention to the importance of preventing bullying, as well as ensure frequent assessment of educators on this dimension during the first two years of employment.

Proactively include all employee groups in antibullying training and reporting practices.

The *t* tests indicate that while we assume that our antibullying initiatives involve the whole school, as Olweus's (1978) original comprehensive school-based program suggested is necessary, the reality is that support staff are not fully included. In fact, one of the keys to successful prevention of bullying—as identified by Creto, Bosworth, and Sailes (1993); Pepler and Craig (1999)—and Shaw (2001)—is a multidimensional approach that includes students, teachers, school staff, and parents. While support staffs are included in the broad category of school staff, only teachers are usually mentioned explicitly. To improve the success of antibullying initiatives, it is important explicitly to include all staff to ensure they have proper training and feel ownership of the problem. All staff need to understand how to intervene in bullying situations and what the communication protocols are. Professional development and ongoing communication with regard to policies and protocols are often a focus at staff meetings; because peripheral staff members are not required to be present at these meetings, they are often not included. It is, therefore, the responsibility of the school administrator to ensure that this information is provided to all members of the school staff and that necessary training and mentoring occur to support their development of skills and depth of knowledge.

Conduct school self-evaluations.

As discussed in Chapter 3, the data indicate that educational professionals are unaware of where bullying occurs. Each school will have different bullying "hot spots" depending on its physical configuration and therefore will need to evaluate its own hot spots. This should be done in two ways. Educational professionals need to be challenged to walk the school differently, looking at it through the eyes of the students. It is my observation that educational professionals often travel the same routes at the same times and therefore see only a small fragment of the interactions that occur. When they change routes to and from their classroom, washroom, staff room, and other areas within the school and vary the times at which they travel throughout the school, a very different picture emerges. It would also be beneficial to have educational professionals from other schools walk the hallways to gain a completely different perspective. Based on the research of Epp and Epp (1998), I also suggest that having students indicate on a school map where bullying occurs may provide valuable information when combined with the observations of the educational professionals in the building.

It is important that once bullying hot spots are identified, they are targeted at all times, and especially during supervision times, by educational professionals. There should be no area of the school that is known to be "teacher-free" and, therefore, a safe place to bully. Furthermore, the hot spot assessment should occur several times throughout the year, as areas vulnerable to bullying behavior will move in response to the heightened awareness.

Share accurate and up-to-date information with all members of the school community.

What is known about bullying has evolved over the past 30 years; however, our internal beliefs may not reflect this evolution. Deconstructing the myths of bullying is a challenge that cannot successfully be addressed in one conversation. The conversation around the theoretical aspects of bullying must be continuous.

Mayer, Caruso, and Salovey (1999) demonstrated that a close link exists between a person's emotional intelligence and his or her ability to cope with environmental demands and uncertainties. Emotional intelligence and one's underlying belief system are important factors. Thus, emotional intelligence has come to be viewed as a predictor of a person's ability to succeed academically and professionally (Parker, Summerfeldt, Hogan, & Majeski, 2004; Taylor, Parker, & Bagby, 1999; Zeidner, Matthews, & Roberts, 2004). Developing an awareness of the complexity of the phenomenon may lead teachers to become "more vigilant and responsive to bullying problems which, in turn, may give children more confidence to seek teachers' assistance when bullying occurs" (Atlas & Pepler, 1998, p. 94).

It appears that regardless of the individual person's starting point, these competencies and beliefs are malleable and can be developed and enhanced via appropriate training and intervention (Bar-On, 1997; Mayer et al., 1999). Analysis of the data suggests that continual education will be necessary for those staff members who hold incorrect assumptions but will be beneficial for all other staff as well.

I also recommend that accurate information must be shared among all staff members with regard to current situations within the school. Everyone needs to be aware of who is currently exhibiting bullying behaviors and who is being victimized. This information is essential so that all school staff members can heighten their observations when those students are involved. Although a balance must be maintained between preserving privacy and giving out information, editing information may create an opportunity for bullying to continue.

Establish a clear protocol regarding the reporting of bullying incidents.

Given the data that shows educational professionals don't know what to do or whom to talk to about bullying, putting in place a clear reporting protocol is necessary. Since each incident will be different, a clear skeleton of guidelines is more useful than a cookie-cutter approach. Davis (2005) found that it is essential that all bullying be reported to a central person, following a consistent format, to ensure that negative behaviors are dealt with consistently, to ensure that a big picture of each student's behavior emerges, and to emphasize the importance of the matter. This is not to say that the person witnessing the behaviors should simply report the incident and not become involved. In addition to documentation of the behavior, follow-up communication must occur with the parents or guardians, explaining the current consequences and the escalating consequences for future behaviors, as well as the classroom teacher and the remainder of the staff to ensure that all stakeholders have current and correct information.

Once the communication protocol has been developed and vetted through the Safe School Team and the staff as a whole, the administrator should make personal contact with peripheral staff members. The principal should ensure that they understand that they are included in this protocol and that they are expected to report incidents of which they are aware. I recommend that the protocol also be communicated with the parent community either via school council (parent teacher association) meetings or in a monthly newsletter. Finally, information about how bullying is reported and to whom it is reported should be shared with students. The communication protocol should be transparent to increase everyone's awareness and accountability.

Develop a schoolwide behavioral rubric that includes predictable and escalating consequences for behaviors.

In conjunction with the communication protocol, a behavioral rubric needs to be developed. Like the reporting protocol, this should be a skeletal guideline, as not every case is the same. Just as we have seen improvement in academic achievement when grading rubrics are provided in advance, we may see a decrease in negative behaviors when explicit expectations and consequences are shared in advance with all stakeholders. It is important that the consequences are not only punitive but also restorative and reflective in nature in order to begin to modify behavior (Davis, 2005). The person chiefly responsible for assigning consequences should find this rubric helpful, as it will be developed in a group setting and incorporate the collective wisdom of all the stakeholders. Teachers, students, and parents should all understand what consequences are going to be assigned to alleviate concerns over potential bias.

Provide support and apply pressure as needed.

I suggest that administrators must be clear about their expectations regarding bullying intervention, and they must communicate them clearly to all stakeholders. Once their expectations are clearly communicated, they will need to both provide support and apply pressure (DuFour, 2004) to the stakeholders as necessary to ensure that expectations are met. Educational professionals may require supports in the form of training, as mentioned in step 1, and pressure, in the form of a conversation or redirection, if they are seen as not intervening or reporting behaviors appropriately. DuFour stated that without pressure, change will not occur despite training and the best intentions. Furthermore, accountability is essential to change old habits into better practice (Hulley & Dier, 2005). I suggest that it is therefore necessary for school administrators to include antibullying practices in formal and informal teacher performance appraisals.

Institute clear policy and protocol to protect the rights of the educational professional.

It is important that educational professionals understand their rights and self-advocate when necessary. I recommend that these rights should be shared with all educational professionals on a yearly basis by their appropriate unions, the school board, and the site administrator. Emphasizing and reviewing these rights will support educational professionals when they are faced with a situation in which they are not treated fairly.

Provide support for and counsel staff who are victimized.

The long-term effects of bullying are just as detrimental for adults as they are for children or youth. Educational professionals who are victimized in their own schools by colleagues, parents, or students need empathy and understanding, just as victimized students do. This support can be difficult for administrators to provide within Ontario as union protocols must be followed. For example, the protocol of not making a negative complaint against a colleague can force the victim to confront the bully directly before seeking support from the administrator. This can be very challenging for the victims, and, therefore, the cycle often continues. In Ontario, therefore, administrators need to find a balance between having an open-door policy and listening on one hand and respecting the boundaries set by the Elementary Teachers' Federation of Ontario, the Ontario English Catholic Teachers' Association, or the Ontario Secondary School Teachers' Federation. Similar restrictions may exist in other jurisdictions.

Bullying is characterized as occurring when there is an imbalance of power, and in the teacher-student relationship the teacher is assumed to have the power (James Matsui Research, 2005). When the situation is reversed, the educational professional may be embarrassed to admit that a student has taken the power in the dyad. This form of bullying should be taken seriously, and the consequences for the bully should be consistent with the school behavior rubric but may require a more severe approach in order to reestablish the power dynamic and restore the teacher's confidence.

The data from my research suggest that perhaps the most difficult scenario to deal with is when a parent bullies an educational professional. The data reveal that all groups of educational professionals have experienced either verbal or physical bullying from parents. Parents are not required to abide by school rules and are not affected by school consequences, such as detentions. It is therefore important that administrators provide educational professionals with not only physical support but emotional support when these situations occur. The administrator can be present at all parent meetings, and in the case of volatile parents, the administrator or a secondary educational professional should be present during formal and informal interview situations. The administrator can also role-play potential scenarios with the educational professional so that staff members can practice responses to diffuse the situation in a safe manner. It appears that is also important for the educational professional and the administrator to remember that while school rules do not apply directly to parents, societal ones do and the police are also members of the school community. What is defined as "verbal bullying" when discussing students is termed by Craig and Pepler (2002), and the police, as verbal harassment or assault. The same is the true of physical bullying, which under the law is physical harassment or assault.

In cases where the victimization is affecting the educational professional's ability to perform his or her duties, feel safe, remain unbiased and fair, or move beyond an experience, counseling is a logical intervention. Most school boards provide an employee assistance program, and when necessary educational professionals are encouraged to speak with a counselor regarding possible solutions.

Provide positive reinforcement for good interventions.

This is a crucial step that can often be overlooked by school administrators. As DuFour (2004) stated, both pressure and support are necessary to create change. The final aspect of support that will help to consolidate the change is to acknowledge change when it is seen in action. It is essential that educational professionals are recognized when they handle a situation correctly and intervene with success. This will allow them to know that their actions have been noticed and their effort has been validated, thereby increasing their confidence in themselves to intervene in future situations. Such recognition will also increase trust in the administration, which will support better rapport and communication. It is important for administrators to remember that validation must refer to specific actions taken by the educational professional to be effective. Simply saying, "Thank you" or "Good job" is not explicit enough to support continued change and best practices. Just as it is important to acknowledge positive and proactive steps taken by educational professionals, it is equally important to acknowledge when parents or students make positive steps forward. Explicit and specific praise is the final stage in the consolidation of changed practice (DuFour).

ENHANCED REALITIES

Each change that we make to our current practice is full of potential to create an enhanced reality for our students. There is no magic elixir or one-step fix to the problems of bullying. The only thing that we know doesn't work is what we are currently doing. Change is our only option.

CASE STUDY: WHERE DID THINGS GO WRONG?

In this case study you examine some of the students and scenarios seen earlier in the book to determine what is needed to enhance their reality. Each behavior or action is as a result of something that is missing. Look at each scenario and try to figure out what character attribute is missing. Think about how you would proactively incorporate character education into your role with students.

1. *Evan is a Grade 1 student who has difficulty maintaining his personal space and is constantly making physical contact with his classmates. Behaviors are beginning to evolve to include sexual touching and sexual comments.*

2. *Cliff is a Grade 3 student with ADHD who is always at the office for being disrespectful and rude to staff and students. He requires one-on-one assistance to make safe choices and frequently hits, punches, kicks, or bites his classmates.*

3. *Spencer is in Grade 9 but has become a nonattender. He is polite to the adults but is sexually degrading in his interactions with female students. He has not crossed a physically abusive line but refers to them as "sluts" and "whores."*

4. *Pauline is a high-achieving Grade 12 student. Pauline started her own website last year called YouCanBeMyDaddy.com and has been providing both online and in-person services to men.*

ACTION: CHARACTER COUNTS

Warm-Up Activity:

Have staff do a "flip-flop" activity to start the conversation on how negative bullying behaviors correlate with the character traits that are valued by your staff. In a flip-flop activity, two staff members bounce their ideas back and forth using one- or two-word answers. Each pair takes a character trait and then does a flip-flop brainstorm to come up with as many correlated behaviors as they can.

Main Activity:

Look back at the behaviors your staff indicated as concerning through the "dotmocracy" activity (see Chapter 4) and determine what type of positive character traits need to become a focus in your school. Once these are identified, have the staff determine how they want to "prime" the students on these positive traits.

(Continued)

(Continued)

Exit Activity:

Each staff member needs to submit a three- to five-sentence written commitment that describes how they will focus on educating their students about the behaviors your school wants to see.

Follow-Up Activity:

The Safe School Team is encouraged to incorporate the behaviors and their correlated positive character traits in a communication pamphlet for parents and students.

SECTION III

Post-Bystanderism

Closing the Circle of Communication

GEN XERS ARE PARENTS NOW

In some ways I'm a classic Gen Xer, and in other ways I'm nothing like the stereotypes that define the generation born between 1961 and 1981. Generation X has aged, and we are now the parents of our students. I say aged despite the fact that my friends and I are still fairly convinced that we haven't grown up. As a whole, we are unlike any generation that has come before us. As a group, we spent our 20s being overeducated and underemployed. We were raised to expect the same lifestyles as our parents and were sadly disappointed when our realities fell short.

As parents, we are a very complicated group with students in every grade from high school down to junior kindergarten and children who haven't yet entered school. We were raised in the time of Pong and Walkmen, not Wii and iPods. That said, we have become mostly tech savvy and "tweet" along with our children. We watched our parents get divorced and were the first generation of latchkey kids with weekend parents. We became self-sufficient and learned how to play mom and dad against each other better than previous generations. We all vowed not to make the same mistakes our parents made. We didn't. We made newer and much more interesting mistakes.

If you were to meet me for the first time, you would be able to run down the checklist of stuff without any difficulty. House—check, kids—check, husband—check, dogs—check, job—check . . . the list goes on and on. However, as my generation is also aware, the story behind the story, à la *Desperate Housewives*, is much more interesting. I'm fairly certain that my autobiography will read, "I married a gay, alcoholic pizza delivery boy," but that's another book entirely.

My mother's generation still doesn't feel comfortable returning items to stores, yet Walmart and other retail giants taught my generation that if I'm not happy, all I have to do is complain. In fact, I can even complain if I don't feel my complaint was taken seriously. As a consumer, I have known that I have a voice since I was a teenager. As an adult, I become downright incensed if I don't get good service whether at a restaurant, a bank, or anyplace else. We Gen Xers are not intimidated by much, and we learned very quickly that we have a voice and as a result demand our rights when we have complaints.

What does this mean for schools? It means that you are dealing with parents who are antiestablishment and somewhat disillusioned with the school system. As students themselves, they followed all the rules, yet the good grades and postsecondary degrees did not deliver the life they promised. It means that you have educated, perhaps overeducated, perhaps more educated than you are, parents who do not understand that schools are not a service industry. If they are not happy with a response, they are very quick to move up the ladder and continue complaining until they feel heard.

IT TAKES A VILLAGE

Being a parent is one of the hardest jobs. Raising our young to become good, ethical, productive, caring, and loving adults is beyond a full-time job. The multigenerational family is one way of providing many positive adults in a child's life. More and more grandparents are taking active roles in raising their grandchildren. Grandma is no longer a little white-haired old lady whom you visit a few times a year. She is often now a fit and energetic woman who sees her grandchildren on a weekly, if not daily, basis. With increased life expectancy and better overall health, this generation of grandparents is healthy and plays an active role in their grandchildren's lives. While this is great for the kids, communication with multigenerational families can prove to be challenging for schools. For instance, what information is grandma or grandpa entitled to? School has changed dramatically since the grandparents or even their children were in school. How do explain our "new" curriculum and expectations to a generation that believed in the value of rigor? In some cases the grandparents, despite living with or near their children and grandchildren, cannot communicate in English. How do you bridge that communication gap?

Nontraditional families are also more the norm than the nuclear family of the past. Whether the family has two moms, two dads, a single parent, a grandparent as parent, or an interracial or interfaith couple as parents, families are all unique and different. The days of the "family tree" are gone, and we now have the generation of students who have "family constellations" to explain all the relationships in their lives. Again, contemporary family arrangements need to be considered when communicating with parents in a bias-free and respectful manner.

Finally, the school itself becomes the village for a lot of our students. Think back to the self-reflection activity in Chapter 7. Research has shown that it is it better to be from a bad family in a good neighborhood than to be from a good family in a bad neighborhood (Elliott et al., 2006). Schools need to become the "good neighborhoods" for all our students. Peer influence, adult influence, and locational influences converge in schools. Our villages have to become the equalizer for our students who do not have ideal home lives. Their education can change their lives, and consequently our society, for the better. Schools need to become all the things that homes sometimes are not. That is a monumental task, but it begins with safety. Our village must be physically and emotionally safe for all our students.

THE APPLE AND THE TREE

I don't think there is an educational professional out there who has not had the "Aha!" moment upon meeting the parents of most students. Never failing, the apple does not fall far from the tree. That can be a great thing when you meet the parents of some of your fabulous students, and it can be enlightening when you finally make contact with the parents of your at-risk students. If the saying proves true and this next generation is in any way similar to its Gen X parents, our communication practices and policies better evolve quickly. I don't want my school to be a Walmart, but I'm beginning to envision the melding of the service industry and our schools. "Hello and welcome to Dawnview. How can I help you?"

CASE STUDY: COMMUNICATING WITH STAKEHOLDERS

In this case study, examine the scenario presented to determine who the stakeholders are. Once you have identified the stakeholders, determine what type of communication is needed and what you would say to the different people involved.

Scenario 1: A Grade 1 boy named Chris has been brought to your office for a second time today for kicking and hitting another student. Chris has received various consequences in the past, including time-outs and not being allowed to go out in the yard during recess. Today he has been given a hula hoop, which he must remain in at all times, to help him develop a clearer understanding of his personal space.

Scenario 2: A Grade 11 boy named James has been being bullied by several members of the school football team. James has reported that he has been receiving hateful text messages and has now been threatened via text. You have a copy of the text messages, and they are clearly unacceptable. James does not want you to involve his parents because the threats are homophobic in nature and he has not come out to his father.

Scenario 3: A group of Grade 8 girls has been brought to your office for making racial comments. They have been making derogatory comments about people of Chinese heritage. They were not making the comments to anyone specifically.

ACTION: COMMUNICATION 101

Warm-Up Activity:

Find your school's communication plan and review it. Highlight good points in green to indicate that they should remain. Highlight in yellow areas that need revision but have potential. Black out any items that need to be removed from your plan.

Main Activity:

You had me at "Hello."

Have a group of educational professionals brainstorm all the communications opportunities that occur during the school year. Consider those opportunities that occur daily, weekly, monthly, and yearly. Put out four pieces of paper with the titles "Daily," "Weekly," "Monthly," and "Yearly" and have the staff do a "sticky note pileup." Individuals write down the communications that they can think of on a sticky note and pile them onto the appropriate paper. All similar sticky notes are grouped within categories, and the ones that are different are then discussed until a consensus is reached. Once consensus is reached, the types of communication should then be further subdivided into proactive and reactive.

Use every opportunity to communicate your messages.

Using the different communication opportunities determined in the first exercise, have staff brainstorm how to use those opportunities to share the school's beliefs regarding bullying and what type of environment they want to have in school. Examine all forms of communication and how messaging can be included proactively. Also consider the effectiveness and methodology behind your reactive messaging.

Develop communication frames.

As a staff, determine the key messages that you need to share effectively and consistently with the extended school community. Develop some communication frames around the key messages and script them. Communication frames are also very useful for staff when they intervene in bullying episodes. When all staff members are supported by having scripted words, they have more chance of intervening effectively. The consistency of the message from all staff will also improve the consistency of messaging for both staff and students.

Exit Activity:

Have staff think about what they are going to change in their proactive and reactive communication with students and parents with regard to bullying and character education.

Follow-Up Activity:

The follow-up activity for the Safe Schools Team is to collate all the different types of communication discussed and begin to determine how to make communication with parents and other caregivers more effective. Your staff may wish to examine the customer service practices in other sectors and determine if any of those practices can be integrated into your school's communication.

Final Thoughts

Change is hard, and figuring out how to deal with bullying differently is a process. It requires change on an individual, a systemic, and a societal level. This can be an overwhelming prospect, so this book is designed to address the small steps that we can take to move as individuals, as a system, and as a society along the Continuum to Action.

To move from inaction to action can require different motivation and thinking for every individual. Some educational professionals will move sequentially, while others may move back and forth as they grow in their understanding. The three areas on the continuum are guidelines to identify diagnostically your current status, to assess your progress formatively, and to determine summatively your success as an intervener.

To be able to notice that something unusual is going on, do the following:

- Reflect on your own perceptions to be sure that your are not allowing your own biases to influence your actions.
- Be present. In the routine and rush of the day, it is easy to slip into "autopilot." Change your timing and pathways around the school and proactively be present in your interactions throughout the day.

To make the rapid decisions needed to act in the moment, do the following:

- Prethink about where your line in the sand is. Self-reflection around what you value and what behaviors you expect will make it easier to determine how you will react when they are not occurring.
- Understand your responsibilities with regard to the students in your class and the students in the school as a whole.
- Develop a clear understanding of the responsibility to supervise students and prethink clear statements that you can use to communicate with students, peers, and parents.
- Understand the language of bullying and the language of character education.

To complete the cycle of intervention, do the following:

- Close the communication gap by ensuring that everyone involved in the situation has had a chance to be heard and has had his or her needs addressed clearly.
- Don't forget to check in with the students involved in the near future to ensure that the issue is resolved and that everyone continues to feel safe.

Again, addressing bullying and bystanderism is a long and involved process. Therefore, a quick jump-start is great way to begin to feel a sense of progress right away. So I'm ending this book with something you can start immediately—something you can try the next time you encounter a bullying episode.

Traditionally, when we as educators observe a bullying interaction, we have private conversations with everyone involved and try to protect everyone's confidentiality. This is not working. Our future adults are not seeing what an active intervention looks like. Intervention is not being modeled for them, and as a result they are not learning how to intervene and stop bullying. We teach our students every day through our words and our actions. They watch everything we do, so we need to model for them how to be an active intervener and how to speak up for themselves and others.

Being an active intervener is not easy the first time you speak out. Even when you know that you're right, and that what you saw was wrong, it is hard to be public in your intervention. But the three minutes outlined below are life changing, both for you and for all the students around you.

HOW TO INTERVENE ACTIVELY IN BULLYING EPISODES IN THREE MINUTES OR LESS

1. **Stop the bullying episode immediately with your words.** Say what you need to say clearly and publicly. Be sure that everyone hears you stop and denounce the behavior; you want them to receive a clear message. Onlookers will realize your expectations and will see intervention modeled. They will also understand that they are safe and protected when they are at school.

   Sample response: Steven, you need to stop what you are doing and make better choices.

2. **Label the unacceptable behavior clearly.** You, as the educational professional, need to define clearly and label the unacceptable behavior for the bully, the bullied, and for all the bystanders who are watching. Identify the behavior without labeling the victim.

Sample response: Steven, you are using inappropriate language and your comments are [ethnic, homophobic, gender-based, etc.] bullying.

3. **Expand your intervention.** This is where you and your colleagues all make similar statements referring to your expectations. You can also use this statement to broaden the bullies' understanding of whom their actions affect.

Sample statement: Our school does not tolerate any type of bullying. We, at this school, do not bully each other. Bullying is hurtful to everyone.

4. **Insist the bullying actions change.** This is where you direct your statements only to the bully but still speak loudly enough for everyone to hear. Tell the student clearly that his or her behavior needs to change immediately, even if the student was "just joking." Direct the student to the office, if the behavior warrants, for further follow-up.

Sample statement: Steven, you need to stop verbally bullying students. Your choices are not appropriate. Please go to the office so that we can discuss the consequences of your choices. [Turn to the victim and the onlookers.] If this continues, please come and tell me. We want everyone in this school to be safe and respected.

SOURCE: Adapted from Lesbian, Gay and Bisexual Youth Program, Central Toronto Youth Services Rainbow Resource Centre, Winnipeg, Canada, 2002.

Resource A: Creating a Culture of Action

Breaking the Bystander Cycle: Moving Education Professionals From Bystander to Intervener[1]

"It's not hatred that kills people, it is indifference."

—Elie Wiesel

While bullying has been an acknowledged problem in schools for the past 30 years, it has become an epidemic in the last decade. Research on the topic has expanded from simply examining the relationship between the bully and the victim to investigating the role of the school community in dealing with this societal issue. Definitions around who and what defines a bully and a victim have also changed. The identification of a third role, that of bystander, has also evolved from past study findings. This particular concept is so recent that it has not yet developed further than defining the bystander as simply the peer group.

The ramifications of bullying can be devastating for all involved. The bully, the bullied, and the bystander, regardless of their age, race, or social status, are all affected. Schools throughout Canada are implementing antibullying programs in an attempt to address the issue. Nevertheless, despite the implementation of programs such as Tribes and LionsQuest, the development of character education programs, the introduction and recent revisions of the Safe Schools Act (2007), and increased public awareness, bullying in schools has not yet been eradicated.

---

[1]This article originally appeared in the fall 2008 issue of the *OPC Register, 8*(3).

The research project upon which this article is based follows the release of statistics from research conducted by Craig, Pepler, and Atlas (2000). Their findings were some of the first to identify education professionals as "bystanders," whether consciously or subconsciously so. Their observations indicated that teachers intervene in only 14 percent of classroom bullying episodes and 4 percent of playground episodes. These numbers were staggering, leading me to wonder how this could be possible. Former and current studies have consistently indicated that in order to prevent bullying, all stakeholders, including the bystander, need to be engaged.

Bystander behavior has become a focal point for a number of programs focused on breaking the bullying cycle (Jeffrey, Miller, & Linn, 2002). Moreover, the term *bystander* needs to be redefined to include not only peer groups but anyone—including education professionals—who remains passive when observing an act of bullying. The purpose of this study was to examine how underlying attitudes and beliefs can directly influence the role an education professional plays in bullying episodes within the school.

THE SCIENCE AND THE THEORY

Research Objectives

This project began with a desire to explore bullying from a less common perspective and delve more deeply into the ideas Craig et al. (2000) brought forward regarding the roles of teachers with respect to bullying. Their qualitative findings identified the educator as a potential bystander in both the classroom and the schoolyard, adding yet another layer to the already complex issue of bullying in schools. Their findings, however, did not address the question of "why" such a conclusion was drawn. This project examined "why" through a set of specific research objectives. My goal was to determine what attitudinal and structural barriers keep education professionals within the bystander role.

Responses were further examined to determine if the bystander role was impacted by factors such as gender, years of experience, or current teaching division. The process included reviewing current literature; creating, analyzing, and modifying a pilot survey; and analyzing the responses of the survey completed by staff in the Bluewater District School Board, Ontario, Canada. The most important objective was to recommend a practical plan to increase the intervention of educators in bullying episodes.

As part of the project, specific research objectives were carried out. These included the following elements:

- Reviewing published literature regarding bullying to describe the evolution of bullying and the role of educators
- Analyzing data collected during the pilot survey to eliminate any ambiguous, negative, or unduly leading statements
- Studying data from participants in the Bluewater District School Board to gain an understanding of educators' perceptions of bullying and to determine what barriers exist that prevent active intervention in bullying episodes
- Determining whether the barriers identified above were affected by gender, years of experience, or current teaching division
- Recommending practical schemas based on the data and suggesting future topics for research with the goal of improving antibullying programs in Ontario.

Procedure

Collection of data began with the creation of a survey questionnaire. The survey was developed in January 2007 by compiling ideas and stylized questions from a variety of previously written surveys (Epp & Epp, 1998; Craig et al., 2000; Hymel, White, & Ishiyama, 2003; Olweus, 1993; Smith, Cousins, & Stewart, 2005). The Bluewater group, acting as our sample, included all school-based employees. All staff members (teachers, education assistants, custodians, office professionals, and administrators) were given the opportunity to participate in the study.

The outline for the study was explained to the participating principals during the monthly administrators' meeting. Fifty-nine administrators were presented with a project overview and given the opportunity to ask questions. Instructions were provided to the principals regarding their roles, as well as what information needed to be passed on to staff. While participation in the research project was voluntary, the principal researcher and the director of education for the Board encouraged staff to take part. School administrators were also directed to include their office professionals, custodial staff, education assistants, and themselves in the project.

The survey was available online with a link provided to all staff. All 48 elementary and 11 secondary schools in the Bluewater District School Board participated in the study. The survey took approximately 20 minutes for each participant to complete. The results were automatically available only to me, the primary researcher.

Questions and Correlations

Step 1: Noticing That Something
Unusual or Inappropriate Is Occurring

The majority of the survey questions related directly to the first stage of bystander intervention described by Huston, Ruggiero, Conner, and Geis (1981). The first of the five stages is the recognition that something unusual or inappropriate is occurring.

What became apparent through the survey findings was a general lack of awareness about what occurs in schools on a daily basis and where those incidents physically occur. This lack of knowledge often prevents education professionals from intervening in bullying episodes by stalling the decision-making process.

Step 2: Deciding If Help Is Needed

Once a situation has been defined as unacceptable, the next step in the cycle according to Huston et al. (1981) is that the bystander decides whether help is required or if the situation can resolve itself. Several sections of the survey addressed the issue of underlying beliefs with respect to bullying. Underlying beliefs can be both positive and negative. They are the beliefs that a person has developed throughout the duration of his or her lifetime as a result of personal experience or media influence. Such beliefs are internal biases that many adults believe to be truths.

These underlying beliefs about bullying may influence whether or not the education professional feels that help is warranted in the situation. For example, some people believe that bullying is just a normal part of growing up or that the increase in bullying is a result of increased violence in the media. If, because of their beliefs, they determine that the victim does not require support, school staff will be unable to move from the role of bystander and instead remain stuck at step 2 of the cycle.

The statistics from the survey revealed that 18 statements could be defined as a truth, as a myth, or as being somewhere in between. For example, when the subjects were asked, "If the victims improved their social skills, they wouldn't be bullied," 17 percent of respondents agreed with the statement, while 56 percent disagreed and 28 percent strongly disagreed. Whether the statement is truth, myth, or somewhere in between, it became clear that education professionals do not all hold the same beliefs.

The data showed that, regardless of the statement, some portion of the surveyed population always appears in each of the four (*strongly agree, agree, disagree,* and *strongly disagree*) response categories. The diversity of responses occurred in relation to nearly all the statements.

This suggests that in any given situation, an education professional may not deem that help is necessary and will therefore not intervene as a result of internal beliefs.

Step 3: Feeling a Responsibility to Help

The third step in the decision to intervene in a bullying situation is that the bystander must determine the extent to which he or she has a responsibility to assist (Huston et al., 1981). The data related to this step in the intervention cycle indicated that there were a portion of respondents for each of the response options (*never, rarely, sometimes, frequently, always,* and *not applicable*). Given this information, some education professionals do not believe that intervention is their responsibility and, therefore, will not move beyond step 3 to intervene in bullying episodes, instead remaining bystanders.

Step 4: Having the Ability to Help

When the bystander does decide to intervene, there must be a determination made as to whether or not he or she possesses the appropriate resources to help the situation (Huston et al., 1981). This step was addressed in several areas of the survey.

Survey responses indicated that at least a quarter of the education professionals did not feel they possessed the appropriate skills for intervening. As a result, these individuals were not able to move beyond acting as a bystander when witnessing bullying incidents.

This fourth stage in the decision-making process is perhaps the most challenging. Educators at this stage were able to identify that something abnormal was occurring and that help was required. They understood that they had a responsibility to assist, but they lacked the confidence to do so. As a result, they felt unsafe, unsupported, and victimized and did not feel they had the skills to intervene successfully.

Step 5: Intervening

In relation to intervention, survey data indicated that a number of education professionals were unable to do so. Once the problem was recognized, the decision was made that help was required, and the observer believed that he or she had the appropriate skill set, only then could the individual decide whether or not to assist. Unfortunately, at this stage it can become challenging for education professionals to reach a conclusion, since incidents can occur quickly and without warning, offering little time to think. While one can assume that no one who works with children or young adults would purposefully want physical or emotional harm to occur, the fact remains that some education professionals remain bystanders.

t Test Indications at All Steps

t tests, which are used to determine whether the means of two groups are statistically different from each other, were used to compare responses based on length of employment, gender, and employment position. While study results were limited to a specific school district, general trending information was produced from these tests. Male and female education professionals responded similarly. Also, the length of employment had no apparent effect on the level of intervention. This result is concerning. It appears to tell us two things: that all of the training and inservices offered to board staff have not improved intervention rates and that recent graduates and new employees are not entering the profession with the necessary skills to address the issue of bullying.

The *t* tests further indicated that employment position within schools affects intervention levels in bullying episodes. Custodial staff and office professionals were least likely to intervene in situations or to feel that it was their responsibility to do so.

BEYOND THE SCIENCE AND THE THEORY

The data from this study are only useful if they improve the practice of education professionals to enhance student success. The study has highlighted areas for growth at each stage identified in the bystander intervention cycle. Recommendations put forward, based on the highlighted areas for growth, are intended to move beyond theory into practical actions to change practice within schools.

Since the data indicated a lack of awareness of the prevalence and location of bullying incidents, recommendations for improvement are as follows:

- Expanded in-faculty teacher training
- Proactive inclusion of all employee groups in antibullying training and reporting practices
- Explicit expectations from administrators with regard to supervision standards
- School self-evaluation exercises to determine bullying "hot spots"

To address step 2 in the bystander intervention cycle, I recommend the following:

- Sharing of accurate and up-to-date information with all members of the school community

To move effectively into the third step, education professionals must understand their responsibility in bullying situations. The following suggestions will support individuals who wish to move from the role of bystander to the role of intervener:

- The development of clear protocols regarding the reporting of bullying incidents
- The promotion of a schoolwide behavior rubric, which includes predictable and escalating consequences for behaviors
- Support, in the form of resources and inservices, and pressure, via clear and consistent expectations and formal processes such as the teacher performance appraisal, from the administrative team, as needed

Step 4 is perhaps the most difficult stage to move through successfully, as it deals with both the knowledge base of the education professionals as well as their current personal experiences. To support individuals through this stage of the cycle, the following actions are recommended:

- Clear policies and protocols to protect the rights of the education professional
- Support and counseling for staff who are victimized

To make education professionals feel that their intervention efforts have made a positive difference, school leaders need to provide constructive reinforcement.

Beyond the general recommendations above comes the practicality of implementation and assisted change within our schools. If change does not occur in the school, then it is not a true change. A practical manual, based on the above recommendations, has been produced that focuses on the key indicated areas. Each section is designed to empower the individual and staff members by engaging everyone in the antibullying process. The manual includes warm-up, main, and exit activities, as well as follow-up activities for safe schools committees. There are templates available in the form of black-line masters; variations and extensions of the different activities are included where possible.

This manual, written for school leaders by a school leader, provides support and guides change for education professionals. I know that no two schools are alike and that what works in one school may not work in another. The schema and suggestions are based on general trending information generated from the study and are meant to act as a starting point for further discussion. School leaders are encouraged to consider these ideas and implement them in their school communities, where appropriate.

CONCLUSION

Survey results indicate that education professionals don't always know whether or how to intervene. Different support systems need to be in place at each of the five stages of the bystander intervention cycle to help education professionals make these determinations. Once changes have been put in place, it is important to remember that the process remains cyclical and requires continual reflection and adjustments in order to be successful. The needs of education professionals, as they move through the cycle of intervention, will change over time. Continual instructional updates and supports will be necessary in order to meet the needs of all professionals.

Bullying must be addressed in a systemic manner; the ramifications of bullying in schools is negative for everyone involved. As the culture of the school becomes affected, so too are all the members within that community. Through a multilayered approach of proactively giving students character education and intervening when bullying does occur, the cycle of bullying can be addressed.

Committed leaders must actively develop a shared vision with their staff in order to change the status quo, which is no longer acceptable. Understanding the current status with regard to the structural and attitudinal barriers that inhibit education professionals from intervening in bullying episodes is simply the first step to creating change. A workable plan must be developed, communicated, implemented, and revised as necessary to create best practices and, therefore, a better school climate for the entire community.

To download the manual, *Creating a Culture of Action—Breaking the Bystander Cycle: Moving Educational Professionals from Bystander to Intervener,* please visit the Ontario Principals' Council website (www.principals.ca).

Resource B:
Bullying and You

The Perspective of Educational Professionals

1. Read the following statements and indicate whether you strongly agree (SA), agree (A), disagree (D), or strongly disagree (SD).

	SA	A	D	SD
Bullies have low self-esteem.				
Victims are too sensitive.				
Everyone is capable of bullying.				
If the victims improved their social skills, they wouldn't be bullied.				
Children who are bullied grow up to be stronger and more self-reliant.				
Violence on TV creates violent children.				
Victims can stop the bully if they fight back.				
Large class sizes are responsible for the increase in bullying.				
Bullies are just having fun. They don't mean to hurt anyone.				
Victims usually bring the trouble on themselves.				
Boys bully more than girls.				

(Continued)

(Continued)

	SA	A	D	SD
Bullies don't have any friends.				
Bullying is just a normal part of growing up.				
Physical bullying is more hurtful than verbal bullying.				
Bullies are secure people.				
Bullying toughens you up.				
Bullies come from dysfunctional families.				
Victims should simply ignore the bully.				

2. Based on your personal experience and perspective, indicate the extent to which you agree or disagree with each of the following statements: strongly disagree (SD), disagree (D), agree (A), strongly agree (SA), don't know (DK).

	SD	D	A	SA	DK
The amount of time and resources dedicated to bullying prevention is sufficient to deal effectively with bullying at your school.					
Racial bullying is a serious problem among students in your school.					
There is a high degree of bullying at your school.					
Sexual bullying is a serious problem at your school.					
Gender-based bullying is a serious problem at your school.					
Homophobic bullying is a serious problem at your school.					
Physical bullying is a serious problem at your school.					
Reactive-victim-based bullying is a serious problem at your school.					
Religious-based bullying is a serious problem at your school.					
Cyber bullying is a serious problem at your school.					

	SD	D	A	SA	DK
Social bullying is a serious problem at your school.					
Relative to other priorities, antibullying receives a substantial time and resource commitment.					
Antibullying education is one of the highest priorities in your school.					
Verbal bullying is a serious problem among students at your school.					
Class-based bullying is a serious problem among students at your school.					

3. Based on your personal experience and perspective, indicate how often the various kinds of bullying are brought to your attention: never (N), rarely (R), sometimes (S), frequently (F), always (A).

	N	R	S	F	A
Reactive-victim bullying					
Gender-based bullying					
Verbal bullying					
Religious-based bullying					
Racial bullying					
Cyber bullying					
Social bullying					
Homophobic bullying					
Physical bullying					
Sexual bullying					

4. Indicate all the reasons you would not intervene in a bullying situation. (Check all that apply.)

❑ The students are just jockeying for social position.
❑ The students need to be able to resolve problems on their own.
❑ I didn't want to make things worse.
❑ I can't make kids play together and be friends.
❑ I'm not their parent. It's their job.
❑ It was just teasing not bullying.
❑ It wouldn't have made a difference.

❏ I didn't want to get involved.
❏ I didn't know what to do or whom to talk to.
❏ I told the students to talk to the teacher on duty.
❏ The students involved were not in my class.
❏ I was physically afraid to become involved.
❏ I was not aware of the situation.
❏ The students are friends.
❏ I thought if I intervened I would not be supported.
❏ The person being bullied deserved it. They brought it on themselves.
❏ It was just horseplay and fooling around.
❏ I wasn't the person on duty.
❏ The bullying was happening off property.
❏ The bell rang and I didn't have time.

5. During the past month of school, with what frequency has bullying behavior occurred in the following locations: rarely (R), biweekly (BW), weekly (W), daily (D), don't know (DK)?

	R	BW	W	D	DK
Eating areas/lunchrooms/cafeterias					
Library					
Playground					
Off property away from the school					
Stairwells					
Off property but near the school					
Hallways					
Computer lab					
Washrooms					
During class rotary[*]					
Entrances and exits					
Gym					
Classrooms					
Change rooms/locker rooms					
On the way to school					
School bus					
On the way from school					

[*]As students move between classes

6. Indicate which of the following are true for you. (Check all that apply.)

   ❏ I have been verbally bullied by a parent.
   ❏ I have been physically bullied by a parent.
   ❏ I have been verbally bullied by a colleague.
   ❏ I have been physically bullied by a colleague.
   ❏ I have been verbally bullied by a student.
   ❏ I have been physically bullied by a student.
   ❏ I have ignored bullying behavior.
   ❏ I have verbally bullied a parent.
   ❏ I have physically bullied a parent.
   ❏ I have verbally bullied a colleague.
   ❏ I have physically bullied a colleague.
   ❏ I have verbally bullied a student.
   ❏ I have physically bullied a student.
   ❏ I think my school is safe.

7. Based on your personal experience and perspective, how often do you . . . [never (N), rarely (R), sometimes (S), frequently (F), always (A), not applicable (N/A)]?

	N	R	S	F	A	N/A
Support those who are bullied?						
Try to stop bullying?						
Report incidents to the parents?						
Bully other adults?						
Feel supported in your actions by your colleagues?						
Listen to both sides of the story?						
Discipline those who are bullied?						
Talk openly about bullying?						
Make excuses for those who bully?						

(Continued)

(Continued)

	N	R	S	F	A	N/A
Feel supported in your actions by the parents?						
Report incidents to the office?						
Discipline those who bully?						
Ignore bullying?						
Notice bullying?						
Bully students themselves?						
Report incidents to the police?						
Feel supported in your actions by the police?						

8. What reason(s) do you think other educational professionals (administrators, office professionals, custodians, educational assistants, and teachers) do not intervene when witnessing bullying behaviors? (Check all that apply.)

❐ They didn't know what to do or whom to talk to.
❐ They were not aware of the situation.
❐ They didn't want to get involved.
❐ They weren't the teacher on duty.
❐ It wouldn't have made a difference.
❐ The bullying was happening off property.
❐ It wasn't their job. They weren't the parents.
❐ It was just teasing, not bullying.
❐ They thought the person being bullied deserved it.
❐ They didn't want to make things worse.
❐ The bell rang and they didn't have time.
❐ The students needed to be able to resolve problems on their own.
❐ They thought they would not be supported.
❐ They were physically afraid to intervene.
❐ The students weren't in their class.

9. How often do you observe other educational professionals (administrators, office professionals, custodians, educational assistants, and teachers) . . . [never (N), rarely (R), sometimes (S), frequently (F), always (A)]?

	N	R	S	F	A
Talk openly about bullying?					
Try to stop bullying?					
Discipline those who are bullied?					
Bully students themselves?					
Bully parents?					
Listen to both sides of the story?					
Bully colleagues?					
Ignore bullying?					
Support those who are bullied?					
Notice bullying?					
Make excuses for those who bully?					

10. How much antibullying or harassment programming does your school offer . . .

	Much More	A Bit More	About the Same	A Bit Less	Much Less	N/A
In comparison to 3 months ago?						
In comparison to 1 year ago?						
In comparison to 5 years ago?						

11. Do you feel comfortable in implementing an antibullying or harassment program?

☐ Yes   ☐ No   ☐ Unsure

12. Do you think your colleagues feel comfortable implementing an antibullying or harassment program?

☐ Yes   ☐ No   ☐ Unsure

13. Do you feel safe in your school?

☐ Yes   ☐ No   ☐ Unsure

14. Do you think your colleagues feel safe in your school?

☐ Yes   ☐ No   ☐ Unsure

15. Do you think students feel safe in your school?

☐ Yes   ☐ No   ☐ Unsure

16. Do you think the public feels safe and welcome when entering your school?

☐ Yes   ☐ No   ☐ Unsure

Resource C: Definitions of the Bully, the Bullied, and the Bystander

- Physical Bullies
  - Engage in the least sophisticated type of bullying
  - Engage in the most easily identifiable type of bullying
  - May hit, shove, push, kick, spit at, or beat up others
  - May damage or steal someone's property

- Verbal Bullies
  - Use words to hurt or humiliate another person
  - May engage in name-calling, insulting, and/or constant teasing

- Social or Relational Bullies
  - Convince their peers to exclude or reject a certain person or people
  - Cut the victims off from their social connections
  - Often also engage in verbal bullying, usually through spreading of rumors and/or gossip
  - Set others up to embarrass them

- Cyber or Electronic Bullies
  - Engage in one of the newest forms of bullying
  - May send e-mails, text messages, or pictures that threaten to hurt or embarrass someone
  - May use instant message chat systems to spread rumors and reveal secrets

○ Can assume various identities online

○ Can use MySpace and other social networking websites to upload embarrassing photos from locations such as washrooms and change rooms

- Gender-Based Bullies

  ○ Engage in exclusion or mistreatment based solely on gender

  ○ Make sexist comments or jokes

- Racial/Ethno/Cultural Bullies

  ○ Treat people in a negative manner because of their culture, their racial or ethnic background, or their skin color

  ○ Say negative things about someone's culture, racial or ethnic background, or skin color

  ○ Use derogatory racial terms

  ○ Tell racist jokes

- Sexual Bullies

  ○ Make crude comments or spread rumors about someone's sexual behavior or sexual preferences

  ○ Touch, grab, pinch, or bump someone in a sexual manner

  ○ Make sexual gestures

  ○ Call someone "gay," "fag," or "lesbian" to upset and defame

- Religion-Based Bullies

  ○ Treat someone in a negative manner because of his or her religious beliefs

  ○ Make negative comments about someone's religion

- Reactive Victims

  ○ Straddle a fence between being a bully and a victim

  ○ May at first appear to be the victim but often taunt others into reacting and then fight back and claim self-defense

  ○ Engage in mostly physical acts of bullying

  ○ Are impulsive and react quickly to intentional and unintentional physical encounters

- Passive Victims

  ○ Avoid aggression and confrontation

  ○ Do not elicit help from peers

  ○ Cry easily

  ○ Will not fight back

  ○ Are not assertive

  ○ Are anxious in social situations

- Aggressive Victims (Pepler & Craig, 2000)
  - May behave in ways that may irritate others
  - May tease and taunt others
  - Lack social skills
  - Tend to be aggressive
  - Will often respond to others aggressively

- Bystander (Coloroso, 2003)
  - Stands idly by when bullying occurs
  - Sometimes ignores the bullying; other times joins in
  - Is not innocent in the bullying cycle
  - Is typically defined as a peer

Resource D: Leet Speak Dictionary

Codes Referring to Parents

9—Parents are around

KPC—Keeping parents clueless

P911—Parent alert

PAL—Parents are listening

PAW—Parents are watching

PIR—Parents in room

POS—Parent over shoulder

Codes Referring to Sex

8—Oral sex

1174—Nude club

GNOC—Get naked on cam

GYPO—Get your pants off

IWSN—I want sex now

J/O—Jerking off

TDTM—Talk dirty to me

FMLTWIA—F*** me like the whore I am

DUM—Do you masturbate?

DUSL—Do you scream loud?

Banana—Code word for "penis"

Kitty—Code word for "vagina"

MPFB—My personal f*** buddy

FB—F*** buddy

RUH—Are you horny?

I&I—Intercourse and inebriation

PRON—Porn

Locational Codes

LMIRL—Let's meet in real life

F2F—Face to face

Hate Codes

182—I hate you

ZERG—To gang up someone

HUYA—Head up your a**

Other

143—I love you

ASL—Age/Sex/Location

DOC—Drug of choice

Blue-Jacking

This is when someone takes over your mobile phone using their Bluetooth and has full access to all of your information. The blue-jacker can text, e-mail, or make calls as you, and all of your stored photos and files are accessible.

References

Astor, R. A. (1995). School violence: A blueprint for elementary school interventions. *Social Work in Education, 17*(2), 101–115.

Atlas, R. S., & Pepler, D. J. (1998). Observations of bullying in the classroom. *The Journal of Educational Research, 92*(2), 86–98.

Bar-On, R. (1997). *The Emotional Intelligence Inventory (EQ-I): Technical manual.* Toronto, Canada: Multi-Health Systems.

Banks, R. (1997, April). Bullying in schools. *ERIC Digest.* (ERIC Document Reproduction Service No. ED407154)

Benseman, J., & Comings, J. (2008). Case study: United States. In *Teaching, learning and assessment for adults: Improving foundation skills.* Paris: OECD. Retrieved October 16, 2010, from http://dx.doi.org/10.1787/172224183252

Boulton, M. J. (1997). Teachers' views on bullying: Definitions, attitudes and ability to cope. *British Journal of Educational Psychology, 67,* 223–233.

Braga, A. A., & Bond, B. J. (2008). Policing crime and disorder hot spots: A randomized controlled trial. *Criminology, 46*(3), 577–607. Retrieved October 16, 2010, from http://petermoskos.com/readings/Braga_Bond-2008.pdf

Bullying. No Way! (2009). *Maria Pallotta-Chiarolli.* Retrieved October 16, 2010, from http://www.bullyingnoway.com.au/talkout/profiles/researchers/mariaPallotta Chiarolli.shtml

Canadian Public Health Association. (2004). *CPHA safe school study.* Retrieved October 16, 2010, from http://www.cpha.ca/uploads/progs/_/safeschools/safe_school_study_e.pdf

Coloroso, B. (2003). *The bully, the bullied, and the bystander.* New York: Harper Collins.

Covey, S. (1989). *The 7 habits of highly effective people.* New York: Simon & Schuster.

Cox, T., Griffiths, A., & Rial-González, E. (2000). *Research on work-related stress.* Luxembourg: Office for Official Publications of the European Communities.

Craig, W. M., & Harel, Y. (2004). Bullying, physical fighting and vicitimization. In C. Currie et al. (Eds.), *Young people's health in context: Health Behaviour in School-aged Children (HBSC) study; international report from the 2001/2002 survey* (Health policy for children and adolescents No. 4; pp. 133–144). Copenhagen, Denmark: World Health Organization. Retrieved October 16, 2010, from http://www.hbsc.org/downloads/IntReport04/Part3.pdf

Craig, W. M., & Pepler, D. J. (1997). Observations of bullying and victimization in the schoolyard. *Canadian Journal of School Psychology, 13,* 41–60.

Craig, W. M., & Pepler, D. J. (2002). *Bullying prevention in schools.* Arlington, VA: Ottawa, Canada: National Crime Prevention Centre. Retrieved October 16, 2010, from http://www.publicsafety.gc.ca/res/cp/res/bully-eng.aspx

Craig, W. M., & Pepler, D. (2003). Identifying and targeting risk for involvement in bullying and victimization. *Canadian Journal of Psychiatry, 48*(9), 577–582.

Craig, W. M., Pepler, D., & Atlas, R. (2000). Observations of bullying in the playground and in the classroom. *School Psychology International, 21*(1), 22–36.

Creto, S., Bosworth, K., & Sailes, J. (1993, April). *Promoting peace: Integrating curricula to deal with violence.* Paper presented at the annual meeting of the American Educational Research Association, Atlanta, GA.

Darley, J. M., & Latane, B. (1973). A study of situational and dispositional variables in helping behavior. *Journal of Personality and Social Psychology, 27*(J), 100–108.

Dawkins, J. L., & Hill, P. (1995). Bullying: Another form of abuse? In T. J. David (Ed.), *Recent advances in paediatrics 13* (pp. 103–122). Edinburgh, Scotland: Churchill Livingstone.

Davis, S. (2005). *Schools where everyone belongs: Practical strategies for reducing bullying.* Champaign, IL: Research Press.

DuFour, R. (2000). Community: Change that counts; initiatives must go deeper than baubles on a branch. *Journal of Staff Development, 21*(4). Retrieved October 16, 2010, from http://www.learningforward.org/news/jsd/dufour214.cfm

DuFour, R. (2004). What is a professional learning community? *Educational Leadership, 61*(8), 6–11.

Duncan, R. (1999). Peer and sibling aggression: An investigation of intra- and extra-familial bullying. *Journal of Interpersonal Violence, 14*(8), 871–886.

Elementary Teachers' Federation of Ontario & Ontario English Catholic Teachers' Association. (2006). *Joint brief: Addressing workplace bullying in Ontario.* Ontario, Canada: Authors.

Elliott, D. S., Menard, S., Rankin, B., Elliott, A., Huizinga, D., & Wilson, W. J. (2006). *Good kids from bad neighborhoods: Successful development in social context.* New York: Cambridge University Press.

Epp, J. R., & Epp, W. (1998, May). *Nobody to turn to: Student solutions to peer harassment.* Paper presented at the Canadian Association for Social Work Education conference, Ottawa, Canada.

Epp, J. R., & Epp, W. (2000). *A comparison of the 1997 and 1999 surveys.* Unpublished manuscript.

Family and Children's Aid Services of Waterloo Region. (n.d.). *Help for parents.* Retrieved October 16, 2010, from http://www.facswaterloo.org/html/HelpParentsSupervision.html

Fischer, U., & Orasanu, J. (1999, May). *Say it again, Sam! Effective communication strategies to mitigate pilot error.* Paper presented at the 10th International Symposium on Aviation Psychology, Columbus, OH. Retrieved October 16, 2010, from http://www.lcc.gatech.edu/~fischer/ISAP99.pdf

Freedman, J. (2001, October). *Evaluating the research on violent video games.* Paper presented at the Playing by the Rules: The Cultural Policy Challenges of Video Games conference, University of Chicago Cultural Policy Center. Retrieved

October 16, 2010, from http://culturalpolicy.uchicago.edu/events/conference-2001-video-games.shtml

Gladwell, M. (2005). *Blink: The power of thinking without thinking.* New York: Little, Brown.

Gladwell, M. (2008). *Outliers: The story of success.* New York: Little, Brown.

Hanish, L. D., & Guerra, N. G. (2000). Children who get victimized at school: What is known? What can be done? *Professional School Counseling, 4*(2), 113–119.

Harris, J. R. (1998). *The nurture assumption: Why children turn out the way they do.* New York: Touchstone.

Hazler, R. (1998). Promoting personal investment in systemic approaches to school violence. *Education, 119*(2), 222–231.

Hazler, R. J., Miller, D. L., Carney, J. V., & Green, S. (2001). Adult recognition of school bullying situations. *Educational Research, 43*(2), 133–146.

Hoel, H., Sparks, K., & Cooper, C. L. (2001). *The cost of violence/Stress at work and the benefits of a violence/stress-free working environment.* Geneva, Switzerland: International Labour Organization. Retrieved October 16, 2010, from http://www.ilo.org/safework/info/publications/lang--en/index.htm

Hoover, J. H., & Oliver, R. (1996). *The bullying prevention handbook: A guide for principals, teachers, and counselors.* Bloomington, IN: National Educational Service.

Howard, N., Horne, A., & Jolliff, D. (2002). Self-efficacy in a new training model for the prevention of bullying in schools. In R. Geffner, M. Loring, & C. Young (Eds.), *Bully behavior: Current issues, research, and interventions* (pp. 181–192). New York: Haworth Press.

Huang, L., Stroul, B., Friedman, R., Mrazek, R., Friesen, B., Pires, S., et al. (2005). Transforming mental health care for children and their families. *American Psychologist, 60,* 615–627.

Hulley, W., & Dier, L. (2005). *Harbours of hope.* Burlington, Ontario: Canadian Effective Schools.

Huston, T. L., Ruggiero, M., Conner, R., & Geis, G. (1981). Bystander intervention into crime: A study based on naturally-occurring episodes. *Social Psychology Quarterly, 44,* 14–23.

Hymel, S., White, A., & Ishiyama, I. (2003). *Safe school survey.* Vancouver, Canada: West Vancouver School District of British Columbia.

International Labour Organization. (2003). *Code of practice on workplace violence in services sectors and measures to combat this phenomenon.* Geneva, Switzerland: Author. Retrieved October 16, 2010, from http://www.ilo.org/public/english/dialogue/sector/techmeet/mevsws03/mevsws-cp.pdf

Ireland, C. A., & Ireland, J. L. (2000). Descriptive analysis of the nature and extent of bullying behaviour in a maximum-security prison. *Aggressive Behaviour, 26*(3), 213–223.

James Matsui Research. (2005). *Report: Bullying in the workplace survey.* Toronto, Canada: Ontario Secondary School Teachers' Federation, Elementary Teachers' Federation of Ontario, and Ontario English Catholic Teachers' Association. Retrieved October 16, 2010, from http://www.osstf.on.ca/

Jeffrey, L. R., Miller, D., & Linn, M. (2001). Middle school bullying as a context for the development of passive observers to the victimization of others. *Journal of Emotional Abuse, 2*(2/3), 143–156.

Joong, P., & Ridler, O. (2005). School violence: Perception and reality. *Education Canada, 45*(4), 61–63.

Josephson Institute. (2001). *2000 report card: the ethics of American youth; violence and substance abuse; data & commentary* (Report #1). Los Angeles: Author.

Kallestad, J. H., & Olweus, D. (2003). Predicting teachers' and schools' implementation of the Olweus Bullying Prevention Program: A multilevel study. *Prevention & Treatment, 6*(21), 3–21. Retrieved January 15, 2006, from http://content.apa.org/journals/pre/6/1/21 (no longer online)

Keizer, K., Lindenberg, S., & Steg, L. (2008). The spreading of disorder. *Science, 322,* 1681–1685.

Kelling, G. L., & Coles, C. M. (1996). *Fixing broken windows: Restoring order and reducing crime in our communities.* New York: Touchstone.

Kelling, G. L., & Sousa, W. H., Jr. (2001). *Do police matter? An analysis of the impact of New York City's police reforms* (Civic Report 22). New York: Manhattan Institute for Policy Research.

Levitt, S. D., & Dubner, S. J. (2005). *Freakonomics: A rogue economist explores the hidden side of everything.* New York: William Morrow.

Loeber, R., & Dishion, T. (1983). Early predictors of male delinquency: A review. *Psychological Bulletin, 94*(1), 68–99.

Loeber, R., & Stouthamer-Loeber, M. (1986). Family factors as correlates and predictors of juvenile conduct problems and delinquency. In M. Tony & N. Morris (Eds.), *Crime and justice* (Vol 7, pp. 29–149). Chicago: University of Chicago Press.

Macklem, G. (2003). *Bullying and teasing: Social power in children's groups.* New York: Kluwer Academic.

Martino, W., & Pallotta-Chiarolli, M. (2005). *Being normal is the only way to be: Adolescent perspectives on gender and school.* Sydney, Australia: University of New South Wales Press.

Mayer, J. D., Caruso, D. R., & Salovey, P. (1999). Emotional intelligence meets traditional standards for an intelligence. *Intelligence, 27,* 267–298.

Mishna, F. (2004). A qualitative study of bullying from multiple perspectives. *Children & Schools, 26*(4), 234–247.

Mishna F., Scarcello, I., Pepler, D., & Wiener, J. (2005). Teachers' understanding of bullying. *Canadian Journal of Education, 28*(4), 718–738.

MSN. (2006). One in ten UK teens have been victims of cyberbullying and one in four know someone who's been a victim [Press release]. Retrieved October 16, 2010, from http://www.microsoft.com/uk/press/content/presscentre/releases/2006/03/pr03603.mspx

Nansel, T. R., Craig, W., Overpeck, M. D., Saluja, G., Ruan, J., & the Health Behaviour in School-aged Children Bullying Analyses Working Group. (2004). Cross-national consistency in the relationship between bullying behaviours and psychosocial adjustment. *Archives of Pediatric and Adolescent Medicine, 158,* 730–736.

Nansel, T. R., Overpeck, M., Pilla, R. S., Ruan, W. J., Simons-Morton, B., & Scheidt, P. (2001). Bullying behaviors among U.S. youth: Prevalence and association with psychosocial adjustment. *Journal of the American Medical Association, 285,* 2094–2100.

National Association of School Psychologists. (2001). *Standards for training and field placement programs in school psychology.* Bethesda, MD: National Association of School Psychologists.

Newman, R. S., Murray, B., & Lussier, C. (2001). Confrontation with aggressive peers at school: Students' reluctance to seek help from the teacher. *Journal of Educational Psychology, 93*(2), 398–410.

Nicolaides, S., Toda, Y., & Smith, P. K. (2002). Knowledge and attitudes about school bullying in trainee teachers. *British Journal of Educational Psychology, 72*(1), 105–118.

Nolen, S. B., Ward, C., Horn, I. S., Campbell, S., Mahna, K., & Childers, S. (2007, April). *Motivation to learn during student teaching.* Paper presented at the annual meeting of the American Education Research Society, Chicago.

Northwest Regional Educational Laboratory. (2001). *Schoolwide prevention of bullying.* Portland, OR: Author. Retrieved October 16, 2010, from http://education northwest.org/webfm_send/465

O'Connell, P., Pepler, D. J., & Craig, W. M. (1999). Peer involvement in bullying: Insights and challenges for intervention. *Journal of Adolescence, 22,* 1–16.

Olweus, D. (1978). *Aggression in the schools: Bullies and whipping boys.* Washington, DC: Hemisphere.

Olweus, D. (1993). *Bullying at school: What we know and what we can do.* Oxford, England: Blackwell.

Olweus, D. (1994). Annotation: Bullying at school; basic facts and effects of a school based intervention program. *Journal of Child Psychology and Psychiatry and Allied Disciplines, 35,* 1171, 1190.

Olweus, D. (2001). A critical analysis and some important issues. In J. Juvonen & S. Graham (Eds.), *Peer harassment in school* (pp. 3–23). New York: Guilford Press.

Olweus, D. (2004). The Olweus Bullying Prevention Program: Design and implementation issues and a new national initiative in Norway. In P. K. Smith, D. Pepler, & K. Rigby (Eds.), *Bullying in schools: How successful can interventions be?* (pp. 13–36). Cambridge, England: Cambridge University Press.

Olweus, D., Limber, S. P., & Mihalic, S. (1999). *The Bullying Prevention Program: Blueprints for violence prevention* (Vol. 10). Boulder, CO: Center for the Study and Prevention of Violence.

Ontario Principals' Council. (2007, February 16). School principals establish standards for learning and safety [News release]. *Ontario Principals' Council Register.* Retrieved, October 13, 2010, from http://www.principals.on.ca/cms/documents/News%20release.pdf

Parker, J. D. A., Summerfeldt, L. J., Hogan, M. J., & Majeski, S. A. (2004). Emotional intelligence and academic success: Examining the transition from high school to university. *Personality and Individual Differences, 36*(1), 163–172.

Patterson, G. R., DeBaryshe, B. D., & Ramsey, E. (1989). A developmental perspective on antisocial behavior. *American Psychologist, 44*(2), 329–335.

Pepler, D., & Craig, W. M. (1999). *Aggressive girls: Developmental of disorder and outcomes* (Report #57). Toronto, Canada: LaMarsh Research Centre on Violence and Conflict, York University.

Pepler, D. J., & Craig, W. M. (2000). *Making a difference in bullying* (Report #60). Toronto, Canada: LaMarsh Research Centre on Violence and Conflict, York University.

Pepler, D. J., Craig, W. M., Ziegler, S., & Charach, A. (1994). An evaluation of an anti-bullying intervention in Toronto schools. *Canadian Journal of Community Mental Health, 13*, 95–110.

Rigby, K. (1998). *Bullying in schools and what to do about it.* Markham, Canada: Pembroke.

Rigby, K., & Bagshaw, D. (2003). Prospects of adolescent students collaborating with teachers in addressing issues of bullying and conflict in schools. *Educational Psychology, 32*, 535–546.

Robins, L. N. (1978). Sturdy childhood predictors of adult anti-social behavior: Replication from longitudinal studies. *Psychological Medicine, 8*, 611–622.

Salmivalli, C. (2001). Group view on victimization. In J. Juvonen & S. Graham (Eds.), *Peer harassment in school* (pp. 398–417). New York: Guilford Press.

Schultz, L., & Da Costa, J. (2005). *Research on and evaluation of bullying and anti-bullying: Initiatives and perspectives in the province of Alberta.* Edmonton, Canada: Alberta Education.

Shaw, M. (2001). *Promoting safety in schools: International experience and action* (NCJ 186937). Washington, D.C.: U.S. Department of Justice, Office of Justice Programs, Bureau of Justice Assistance. Retrieved October 16, 2010, from http://www.ncjrs.gov/pdffiles1/bja/186937.pdf

Siann, G., Callaghan, M., Lockhart, R., & Rawson, L. (1993). Bullying: Teachers' views and school effects. *Educational Studies, 19*(3), 307–321.

Smith, J. D., Cousins, J. B., & Stewart, R. (2005). Anti-bullying interventions in schools: Ingredients of effective programs. *Canadian Journal of Education, 28*, 739–762.

Sourander, A., Helstela, L., Helenius, H., & Piha, J. (2000). Persistence of bullying from childhood to adolescence—A longitudinal 8-year follow-up study. *Child Abuse and Neglect, 24*(7), 873–881.

Starr, L. (2000). *Sticks and stones and* names *can hurt you: De-myth-tifying the classroom bully!* Retrieved October 16, 2010, from http://www.peelearlyyears.com/pdf/Sticks%20and%20Stones%20and%20Names%20Can%20Hurt%20You.pdf

Steele, C. M., & Aronson, J. (1995). Stereotype threat and the intellectual test performance of African Americans. *Journal of Personality and Social Psychology, 69*, 797–811.

Stephenson, P., & Smith, D. (1989). Bullying in two English comprehensive schools. In E. Roland & E. Munthe (Eds.), *Bullying: An international perspective* (pp. 22–34). London: Fulton.

Sudermann, M., Jaffe, P. G., & Schieck, E. (1996). *A.S.A.P.: A school-based anti-violence program.* London, Canada: London Family Court Clinic.

Swearer, S. M., Song, S. Y., Cary, P. T., Eagle, J. W., & Mickelson, W. T. (2001). Psychosocial correlates in bullying and victimization: The relationship between depression, anxiety, and bully/victim status. *Journal of Emotional Abuse, 2*, 95–121.

Taylor, G. J., Parker, J. D., & Bagby, R. M. (1999). Emotional intelligence and the emotional brain: Points of convergence and implications for psychoanalysis. *Journal of American Academy of Psychoanalysis, 27*, 339–354.

Texas Department of Family and Protective Services. (n.d.). *Child alone— Frequently asked question[s].* Retrieved October 16, 2010, from https://www.dfps.state.tx.us/Child_Protection/About_Child_Protective_Services/faqchildalone.asp

Townsend-Wiggins, C. (2001). Teachers' perceptions of and interventions in episodes of bullying in schools. *Dissertation Abstracts International A. The Humanities and Social Sciences, 62*(09), 2982. (UMI No. 3027157)

Tuckman, B. (1965). Developmental sequence in small groups. *Psychological Bulletin, 63*(6), 384–399.

Twemlow, S. W. (2001). Modifying violent communities by enhancing altruism: A vision of possibilities. *Journal of Applied Psychoanalytic Studies, 3*(4), 431–462.

Twemlow, S. W., Fonagy, P., & Sacco, F. (2004). The role of the bystander in the social architecture of bullying and violence in schools and communities. *Annals of the New York Academy of Sciences, 1036*, 215–232.

Weinhold, B. K., & Weinhold, J. B. (1998). Conflict resolution: The partnership way in schools. *Counseling and Human Development, 30*(7), 1–2.

Weir, E. (2001). The health impact of bullying. *CMAJ, 165*, 1249.

Wlodkowski, R. (1999). *Enhancing adult motivation to learn: A comprehensive guide for teaching all adults* (2nd ed.). San Francisco: Jossey-Bass.

Zeidner, M., Matthews, G., & Roberts, R. D. (2004). Emotional intelligence in the workplace: A critical review. *Applied Psychology: An International Review, 53*, 371–399.

Index

CORWIN
A SAGE Company

The Corwin logo—a raven striding across an open book—represents the union of courage and learning. Corwin is committed to improving education for all learners by publishing books and other professional development resources for those serving the field of PreK–12 education. By providing practical, hands-on materials, Corwin continues to carry out the promise of its motto: **"Helping Educators Do Their Work Better."**

The Ontario Principals' Council (OPC) is a voluntary association for principals and vice-principals in Ontario's public school system. We believe that exemplary leadership results in outstanding schools and improved student achievement. To this end, we foster quality leadership through world-class professional services and supports. As an ISO 9001 registered organization, we are committed to **"quality leadership—our principal product."**